I thank my Lord and Savior Jesus Christ for the revelations in this book. This was truly an adventure to put these revelations into a meaningful format that can help and guide others. I also want to thank my wife Silke who has the patience of a saint. She allowed me to have the peace and support necessary to bring forth this work. Additionally, I want thank my brother in Christ Pastor Mark Goeglein for his steady hand of support during the writing of this book. He truly was the blessing that I needed to stay focused. And finally I want to thank my good friend and brother in Christ Pastor Craig Bennett who has always encouraged me to be all that I can be for the Kingdom of God. .

TABLE OF CONTENTS

PREFACE

INTRODUCTION

CHAPTER 1 HISTORICAL BACKGROUND

CHAPTER 2 TEMPLES: NOT JUST FOR WORSHIP

CHAPTER 3 THIS LIFE

CHAPTER 4 FREEDOM AND ACCOUNTABILITY

CHAPTER 5 THE LAW, POLITICS, ECONOMICS AND CHRISTIANS

CHAPTER 6 A BETTER UNDERSTANDING

CHAPTER 7 THE NEW TEMPLE SYSTEM

CHAPTER 8 THE NEW FOCUS

CHAPTER 9 THE INTELLIGENT DESIGNER AND GRACE

CHAPTER 10 PROTECTING THE TEMPLE FROM SIN

CHAPTER 11 KEEPING THE TEMPLE CLEAN

CHAPTER 12 LOVE AND LIGHT: A CHRISTIAN'S JOURNEY

CHAPTER 13 THE JOY OF BEING A CHRISTIAN

A NOTE FROM THE AUTHOR

PREFACE

The destruction of objective morality by the world system and Satan cannot be overstated. It directly affects our mind, body and spirit. Our bodies are designed to contain our mind, spirit, soul and a part of our creator, the Holy Spirit. Holiness is a term that conveys a state of cleanliness and objective spiritual morality. Without God's Holy Spirit inhabiting our bodies, we cannot truly know and understand objective morality. This kind of morality is true anytime, anywhere and applies to all. When contrasted with mankind's morality which changes over time, God is the only source that can truly lead us to a life of joy, peace and happiness.

God the creator of our existence designed certain parameters for us to live within. With this knowledge our lives have real purpose and meaning. Because of our interactions with the world system, the purpose and meaning of our lives have become distorted. The world system continually bombards our senses with evil until we are so de-sensitized that some of us lose our identity in Christ. This state of mind is what is known as spiritual amnesia. There are several causes of spiritual amnesia. Jesus describes some of the causes of spiritual amnesia in the parable of the Sower of the seeds. (Matthew 13:1-9)

The vast majority of Christians want to live a clean moral life. Problems develop when trying to integrate into the world system that distorts what is clean and what is moral in God's eyes. Because our minds are constantly under attack by the corruption of the world, we are de-sensitized to the point of not reacting as we should to things that are not clean or moral. This affects our minds and eventually our bodies. Our bodies are Temples of the living God and must be kept holy. (1 Corinthians 6:19-20) This is an extremely difficult task for many people living under the influence of the world system. A discussion of our bodies being Temples of God will be covered later in this book.

This book is an important reminder to all Christians who are suffering from amnesia. The purpose and meaning for our lives are constantly being stolen from our conscious state of mind. The world that we live in distorts our ability to perceive morality objectively. Objective morality is not and cannot be the creation of human design. It must be created from an eternal moral source. Mankind changes morality as it evolves and seeks to justify its behavior by changing what is right and wrong and what is good or bad. Objective morality must be grounded in an eternal spiritual source and authority. There is only one moral authority that we can turn to and trust that is eternal. That eternal objective moral authority is God.

INTRODUCTION

Understanding the mystery of life and its meaning has been the quest of many philosophers and theologians since the beginning of time. Trying to understand this without the knowledge of an all-good, all-powerful God is impossible. The Holy Scriptures are the only road map that we have that provides coherent insight into the mystery, meaning and purpose of life.

There are several passages of scripture that reference God knowing us before we were formed or while we were in our mother's womb. (Genesis 2:7, Judges 13:5, Isaiah 49:5, 43:21,Jeremiah 1:5, Galatians 1:15) All of these passages point to the realization that we were all known by God even before we entered our mother's womb. To be in his presence, we must be holy. When God decided to give us human form he designed something to contain our essence that he could love and fellowship with. Amazingly, he chose dirt! Once we were actualized in dirt through Adam and Eve, we continued to be holy. When they sinned, our flesh and our spirits became unholy.

Why did God choose dirt? This is another part of the mystery of our spiritual journey. Knowing some of the attributes of God provides some insight. Because God is omniscient, he knows all. This is due to his eternal being and attribute of living in the past, present and future simultaneously. His foreknowledge allows him to see the future choices that we will make with our free will. He does not override our ability to choose freely but he does see the choices that we will make in the future. God foresaw the choice that Adam and Eve would make and provided a plan of redemption for them from the beginning.

By knowing that man would be corrupted by sin, God developed a way of escape by letting the body created of dirt, die. The death of the body created another issue that needed to be dealt with. What would happen to the eternal soul that was dwelling in a body that is now dead? How could God redeem something that is eternal that has been corrupted? It would take many centuries and a lot of souls being lost but God never gave up on us. Sin and corruption leads to death. The next step in restoring God's relationship with his creation is revealed by the words of Jesus himself. After throwing the merchants out of the Temple in the book of John chapter 2, the Jews demanded a miraculous sign from Jesus to prove his identity and authority. Jesus answered them saying, "Destroy this temple and I will raise it again in three days."(John: 2:19)

The Jews thought that Jesus was referring to the literal Temple but this was the first reference to our bodies being Temples. After Jesus was resurrected from the dead by the power of the Holy Spirit, he revealed that our bodies are more than just a place for our souls and spirits to dwell. The body was also designed for the spirit of God to inhabit. (Acts 1:1-8) This is the first revelation of the Holy Spirit of God dwelling in the bodies of believers. This is when the Temple system of human beings began. It is up to each believer to keep his or her Temple clean from sin. Just as Satan did in the Garden of Eden, his job continues to be to corrupt and defile our Temples. Many Christians have amnesia. They go to church every week, read their Bibles but forget that we are Temples of the living God and must be set apart from sin and the world.

Understanding that Jesus is God and human allows us to be physically and spiritually related to him. His suffering and sacrifice for us is as a fellow human being, brother and God. The incarnation of Jesus in the flesh allowed him to share and most importantly feel our weaknesses, temptations and fears. His mission was to restore us back into a right relationship with God the Father and destroy the works of Satan. As a part of God's plan of redemption, Jesus had to show us how to resist Satan and the temptations of this world. He demonstrated that it could not be dome with our own strength. There are other elements and tools that God designed for mankind to fight and defeat the works of Satan. Understanding that the new Temple System is one of the main elements of God's plan of redemption is crucial. God's original design had morality built into it for mankind. God is eternal and so is the morality of objective spiritual truth that emanates from his nature. When we view morality as an eternal objective spiritual truth, it cannot be changed to suit the corruption that exists in the minds of men.

Dr. William L. Craig a prominent theologian and author of the website "Reasonable Faith" expressed a fundamental understanding for God's highest level creation, man, in the following excerpt from his website.

Does right and wrong really exist? Before you can determine *what* is right and wrong, you have to know that there really is a right and wrong. What is the basis for saying that right and wrong exist? Is there really a difference between the two? Traditionally the answer has been that moral values are based in God. God is by His very nature perfectly holy and good. He is just, loving, patient, merciful, and generous. All that is good comes from Him and is a reflection of His character. Now God's perfectly good nature issues forth in commandments to us, which become our moral duties, for example, "You shall love the Lord your God with all your heart, mind, and strength," "You shall love your neighbor as yourself," "You shall not murder, steal, or commit adultery." These things are right or wrong based on God's commandments and God's commandments are not arbitrary but flow necessarily out of His perfect nature.

This is the Christian understanding of right and wrong. There really is such a being as God who created the world and made us to know Him. He really has commanded certain things. We really are morally obligated to do certain things (and not to do others). Morality isn't just in your mind. It's real. When we fail to keep God's commandments, we really are morally guilty before Him and need His forgiveness. The problem isn't just that we *feel* guilty; we really *are* guilty, regardless of how we feel. I might not *feel* guilty because I have an insensitive conscience, one that's dulled by sin; but if I've broken God's law, I *am* guilty, regardless of how I feel.

So, for example, if the Nazis had won World War II and succeeded in brainwashing or exterminating everyone who disagreed with them, so that everybody would think the Holocaust had been good, it would still have been wrong because God says it is wrong, regardless of human opinion. Morality is based in God and so real right and wrong exist and are unaffected by human opinions.

I've emphasized this point because it's so foreign to what a lot of people in our society think today. Today so many people think of right and wrong not as matters of *fact*, but as matters of *taste*. For example, there isn't any objective fact that *broccoli tastes good*. It tastes good to some people, but tastes bad to others. It may taste bad to you, but it tastes good to me! People think it's the same with moral values. Something may seem wrong to you, but right to me. There isn't any real right or wrong. It's just a matter of opinion.

Now if there is no God, then I think these people are absolutely correct. In the absence of God everything becomes relative. Right and wrong become relative to different cultures and societies. Without God who is to say that one culture's values are better than another's? Who's to say who is right and who is wrong? Where do right and wrong come from? Richard Taylor, who is a prominent American philosopher and not a Christian by the way, makes this point very forcefully. Look carefully at what he says:

The idea of *moral* obligation is clear enough provided that reference to some lawmaker higher than those of the state is understood. In other words, our moral obligations can be understood as those that are imposed by God. But what if this higher-than-human lawgiver is no longer taken into account? Does the concept of a moral obligation still make sense? He says the answer is "No." I quote: "The concept of moral obligation is unintelligible apart from the idea of God. The words remain but their meaning is gone."

He goes on to say: The modern age more or less repudiating the idea of a divine lawgiver, has nevertheless tried to retain the ideas of moral right and wrong without noticing that in casting God aside, they have also abolished the meaningfulness of right and wrong as well. Thus, even educated persons sometimes declare that such things as war, or abortion, or the violation of certain human rights are morally wrong and they imagine that they have said something true and meaningful. Educated people do not need to be told however, that questions such as these have never been answered outside of religion.

Do you catch what even this non-Christian philosopher is saying? If there is no God, no divine lawgiver, then there is no moral law. If there is no moral law, then there is no real right and wrong. Right and wrong are just human customs and laws that vary from society to society. Even if they all agree, they're still just human inventions. So if God does not exist, right and wrong do not exist either. Anything goes!!

We've seen that these kinds of value judgments cannot be meaningfully made unless God exists. If God does not exist, anything goes including murder, rape, torture, and child abuse. None of these things would be wrong because without God, right and wrong do not exist. Everything is permitted.

So if we want to be able to make moral judgments about what's right or wrong, we've got to affirm that God exists. If God exists, then we cannot ignore what *He* has to say. The correct answer to the question does right and wrong exist is: "I'm nobody! God determines what's right and wrong and I'm just interested in learning and obeying what He says."

This book is written as a part of a continuing series on Christian conduct. The standard for holiness cannot be emphasized enough. It is a requirement that cannot be overlooked by God. Living in a corrupt fallen world is not easy for most Christians. The allure to fit into the world system causes many Christians to forget who they are and how they must conduct themselves. If we do not project the spirit of God who is in us and allow the world to project its' spirits on us, the results can cause our Temples to be defiled and therefore unclean before God.

As we mature into more knowledge and grace, there are certain things that we must do. By understanding who we are, what we are and who we serve, keeping our Temples clean should be a daily routine. Unfortunately for many Christians, integrating into the world system causes amnesia. We quickly forget who we serve and the purpose of our creation. The new covenant outlined in the New Testament of the Bible provides much needed grace for many Christians. Praise God that we are not punished or killed instantly for not maintaining his commandments. In this new covenant there is a process of forgiveness that was not so readily available in the old covenant. The old covenant did have rewards for maintaining God's commandments but there were severe punishments for breaking them. Thank God for his mercy and grace in John 3:16.

HISTORICAL BACKGROUND

The Hebrew story of creation is where we must begin. We must decide to accept it or reject it. The Bible is the Christian reference source for all of reality. For the Christian, there is nothing else. If we decide to reject the Bible as the source of our faith, what follows next? Mankind does not have any other instruction on how to relate to and have a relationship with our creator except through the Bible. Those of us that do indeed accept the Bible as God's inspired word possess a roadmap that will guide us through this life. The Bible is and must be the ultimate authority for all Christians. When we decide to reject portions of the Bible that we deem false and only accept the portions that we agree with, this is not living by faith. Faith in Jesus Christ is the essential element that is at the core of our belief system. The Old Testament chronicles God's relationship with his creation, man. The New Testament provides salvation and a new way of living through a relationship with Jesus. The Bible goes on to provide guidance on how to have a relationship with God. Until the birth, death and resurrection of Jesus Christ, there was very little hope for mankind. Time as we know it started all over again because of Jesus' life here on earth. At the same time God's relationship with mankind started all over again. The New Testament brought a new covenant between God and mankind. This time the relationship between God and mankind included the power to maintain and not break this sacred bond. This power is the Holy Spirit.

For the Christian, the Holy Spirit is a spiritual truth. Not accepting the Holy Spirit as an objective spiritual truth leads to not understanding God's plan of redemption for his people. Let's start again and accept that the story of creation in Jewish history is true. Sin entered the world as described in the Old Testament. Once we see and understand the consequences of sin, we can now have a better understanding of God's relationship with man. In the beginning God and man had a close loving relationship. The creator to creature relationship was more of a parent/ child relationship with God and Adam and Eve. God had a plan for his special creation. It involved Adam having dominion over everything on earth. Once Adam and Eve sinned, they surrendered this dominion over the earth to Satan. This triggered a process to restore the relationship between God and man that would take thousands of years. Now that the relationship between God and mankind has been re-established, there is the possibility that man can join God in the battle to restore the earth back to the original design that God intended.

The reconciliation process involves returning man to the original spiritual condition that God requires of him. Man must now evolve into a spiritual condition known as holiness. Being holy by definition means to be dedicated and devoted to God by being separated from sin. The Bible teaches us that Adam and Eve sinned and were no longer holy. This created a situation that destroyed a loving relationship of trust and honor between God the parent, and his children Adam and Eve. What could God do to restore this relationship to the holy state that he requires?

At this point we must spend some time understanding the character and some of the attributes of God. First, it is important to know that God is a perfect, all-good, all powerful, loving being. He cannot lie or sin. He is the moral lawgiver that has ordained what is right and what is wrong. Also, God is omnipotent (He is all powerful), Omni-present (He is everywhere) and Omniscient (He knows all). It is the Omniscience of God that will provide an understanding of God's design for mankind. It will answer the question of and provide insight into solving the condition of man's sin. God's solution to redeem his creation and restore mankind back to a state of holiness was built into the original plan of creation. (Genesis 3:15) This is the first revelation that God would send Jesus to redeem mankind. God used the people of what we now call the Jewish faith to start the process of reconciliation. They were his chosen people. Things got much worse before they got better because sin and corruption were rampant throughout the world.

The God of the Old Testament was not as forgiving of sin as he is now in the New Testament Church. Sin and corruption were so great before God's eyes, he decided to destroy every living thing on the earth except Noah, his family members and enough animals to restart and repopulate the earth. After all this you would think that things would get better but they did not. Sin and corruption still dominated the hearts of many people after the great flood. God's plan of redemption included a commandment phase to help people return to him. It began with God giving commandments to Moses for his people to follow. The Lord then set up a Holy Priesthood with Aaron and his descendants for God's chosen people. These commandments were designed to keep God's chosen people undefiled by the lusts of the world. The penalties for violating these commandments were extremely harsh. Death was a common penalty for violating a commandment.

During the time period of the Old Testament, sin was dealt with quickly by the Lord. God's requirement for his chosen people to be holy was not negotiable. The Lord did not trust his chosen people to follow his commandments so he only allowed very few people to be in his presence. There was always the fear that God would kill anyone who was not consecrated before coming into his presence. When the center place of worship was established, God dictated exactly how it was to be constructed; the materials used in the construction, the objects and instruments that were to be used in it and most importantly, the ceremony that consecrated and made everything involved holy. The priests that went before the Lord on behalf of the people also had to be consecrated to the Lord and made holy. There was no room for error during any encounter with the living God. Even the priests were subject to instant death if they did not follow God's instructions to the letter.

This was a defining time for God's chosen people. The Bible declares in the books of Exodus and Leviticus that the Lord spelled out numerous laws and the punishments for violating these laws. As Christians, we understand that violations of God's laws are sin and it is sin that separates us from him. We live in an incredible time period in which someone has paid in advance for our past, present and future sins. Jesus Christ is God's answer to sin. Until Jesus died for the sins of the world, justice for sins against God could not be satisfied. Burnt offerings and animal sacrifices could not fully restore man's relationship with God. No one could keep all the commandments that God required to be holy and consecrated to him. We must now unfold another part of the mystery that God designed to reconcile us back to him.

Our God is a God of justice. All sin must be paid for. This presents a serious dilemma for mankind. We are all subject to God's system of justice. Who could pay the price for all the sins that people commit and satisfy God's justice? The Old Testament gives us great insight into the ways of God. Major themes in the Old Testament included purity, exactness, perfection and holiness. According to the Bible, there is not one living being that is capable of having these attributes and qualities. By design God had a solution to this dilemma. Being a Triune God, God possesses the attributes of purity, exactness, perfection and holiness in three persons. As in anything that God does, he does it in agreement with all three parts of his person, the Trinity. A decision was made to satisfy the justice that God required. The decision included the death of one person of the Trinity, Jesus Christ. As a perfect, sinless sacrifice, he was the only one that could satisfy God's requirement for justice. Jesus as God would take on human form, live a sinless life and offer himself as a perfect sacrifice to satisfy God's requirement for justice. By being human and God,

Jesus was able to establish himself as physically related to mankind and could have a sibling relationship with those who would choose to follow him.

When Jesus died and was resurrected, he conquered sin and death for all who would follow him. One of the promises that Jesus made to his disciples and to us is that if we really trust in him, God the Father would send the Holy Spirit to be with us and seal us until the day of redemption, judgment day. Until then, the Holy Spirit dwells in each and every believer. How is this possible? As members of the New Testament Church and the New Covenant with God, we are all now Temples of the Living God, paid for by the blood of Jesus. Believers now have kinship with Jesus and inheritance rights in his kingdom. We are now children of the living God. How do we know this? God's spirit dwells in us and communicates with us.

TEMPLES: NOT JUST FOR WORSHIP

In the Old Testament there were altars built to worship God. Over time portable Tabernacles were constructed for the presence of God to dwell in. These Tabernacles were replaced by a centralized Temple in Jerusalem for God's people to collectively worship and experience his presence. Because of our sins against God, we were required to make continuous sacrifices to him. Our relationship with God was not yet restored. In the Tabernacle setting, very few people were allowed to be in his presence because God would kill those who were not clean in his presence. In the New Testament under grace, we are being prepared to become vessels to carry the presence of God within our bodies. We are now vessels that he can use to bring change to a decaying world. God can use his angels to do a lot of his work but he has also chosen the people created in his image to carry out his Will. As Temples, we are not to be worshipped. We must not be so distracted by the cares of this world that we are not ready when God calls upon us to do his work. An important preparation for this work is to keep our Temples clean. In addition, we must be prepared to serve in the army of the Lord. There is a spiritual war that rages all around us. Because of this we must be ready to fight against those who oppose God's Will. Our Temples are naturally weak. Chapter 6 of the book of Ephesians in the New Testament arms Christians with weapons to do battle with God's enemies. As in any civilization there must be an army to protect and provide security to its citizens and the kingdom of God is no exception.

As Temples of God we have other functions to perform. These primary functions are to serve, praise and glorify him. We are also to be vessels that bring God's blessings to his people and others. An important message that we bring to the world is that love, joy, peace and happiness can only come from the spirit of God. The world system fails miserably in these areas. The main reason why the world fails in these areas is that it is controlled and run by evil. Let us take a look at the fruits of evil? Evil never brings peace. There are no great stories of joy when evil is involved. Anyone trying to experience love and happiness without God can certainly expect to have a bad track record when evil is involved. Look at the condition of the world today. Left to its own morals and values the world would destroy itself. Only through God's grace and his people does the world have any chance of experiencing the fruits of God's spirit.

The Temple system of the New Testament Church is another mystery of God. Being created in his image provides us with a template of his original design. As human beings, we were created with the DNA of our parents. Once we are born again by water and spirit, we take on God's DNA. By keeping our Temples clean and teaching our children and communities God's laws and values, we pass on the purest DNA possible. This is our reasonable service to him. Studying God's people in the Old Testament revealed that it was important that his people not mix with others that did not have the same DNA. The same holds true today. The challenge for us today is the diluting of God's DNA by the integration and corruption that comes with having peace with the world system. So many ministries and Christian denominations have so many different standards that many people cannot decide which ones to follow. This is another tactic used by the enemies of God to keep his people divided.

A major problem for many of us is a lack of understanding regarding the sacraments. Let us take a look at the Lord's Supper or what some refer to as Holy Communion. Some churches deny communion to some of its members based on violations of church doctrine. Others allow anyone to participate in the Lord's Supper. It is difficult to balance these extremes without a thorough understanding of the scriptures. According to Jesus, we should take the Lord's Supper in remembrance of the great sacrifice that he made for all of us. It is a sacrament that demonstrates an active relationship with God. There are strict requirements that must be met in order to participate in this sacrament.

This is what the Bible teaches in 1 Corinthians chapter 11:26-32. "For whenever you eat this bread and drink this cup, you proclaim the Lord's death until he comes. Therefore, whoever eats the bread or drinks the cup of the Lord in an unworthy manner will be guilty of sinning against the body and blood of the Lord. A man ought to examine himself before he eats of the bread and drinks of the cup. For anyone who eats and drinks without recognizing the body of the Lord eats and drinks judgment on himself. That is why many among you are weak and sick, and a number of you have fallen asleep. But if we judged ourselves, we would not come under judgment. When we are judged by the Lord, we are being disciplined so that we will not be condemned with the world".

The scripture reveals that we must take a self -examination of ourselves in order to be in a right relationship with the Lord before participating in the Lord's Supper. Worshipping in an unworthy manner can cause sickness and weakness in us. How can we go to God with a lot of garbage in our hearts? The hatred of others, non-forgiveness, selfishness, greed and a host of others things that make our Temples unclean cause our worship to God to be unworthy. Worship without consecration has little value. We are more than worshippers. By design we should strive for holiness. This is God's will for every Christian. The goal for every Christian is to be transformed into the likeness of Jesus Christ. Remember, we are created in God's image. Because we are created in God's image, he desires us to have a relationship with him that requires us to have a clean Temple.

The next obvious question that comes to mind is this. Are you a Christian that has the responsibility to keep your Temple clean? It is amazing how many people believe that they are Christians. They truly believe that going to church and being a good person by the world's standards are enough to be a Christian. There is a vast difference between the moral standards of God our creator and the world.

Every day we are faced with choices that will please God or please the world. How can we say that we are Christians if the majority of our choices go against God and support the world? It is really that simple. Christians should not support the things of the world that cause our Temples to be unclean. Do we choose God and his righteousness or do we choose what the world desires? Because God requires us to be holy, our choices should reflect that we are holy.

In my travels I speak to a lot of people that claim to be Christians but do not know that they are required to be holy. They do not realize that being a Christian means to become a Temple of the living God and having the responsibility to keep it clean. Holiness is an extreme form of cleanliness. No one can achieve this by their own actions. It must be acquired through having a relationship with Jesus Christ and taking on his righteousness. It is our faith in Jesus that makes us holy Temples. Keeping our Temples clean becomes both our responsibility and privilege.

When we as Christians take on the values of the world, we become unclean before God and must repent of our actions. This is why we must continually renew our minds with the word of God to cleanse us of the world's influence and values. Be aware that it is Satan's mission to make us unclean before God. Because we have free will and choose the things of the world that makes us unclean before God, it cannot be said that we are living in a manner that is pleasing to him. In fact the choice of worldly living makes us unholy before God.

This is a good time to differentiate between those who are living a Christian life and those who only give lip service to being a Christian. The Bible is our road map. Let us consider this. Are we all not made in God's image? Yes. Are we all brothers and sisters in Christ? No. This is where the trouble begins. According to the scriptures we all belong to the Lord. (Romans 14:8) By choosing not to live by God's standards, you cannot claim to be a Christian. Being a Christian is not a part-time activity. It requires going through the sanctification process which is being set a part from the world and devoted to God.

The world is filled with people who claim to be Christians but their lifestyle choices reveal a different reality. The lives of many of us mirror that of non-Christians. We are involved in the same activities as the enemies of God. For the sake of peace with the world we accept and live with things that defile our Temples.

It is interesting to find that people who claim to be Christians supporting many of the sins that put them at odds with God. Some of us support abortions on demand, gay and lesbian lifestyles; belong to racist organizations; lie on a constant basis, cheat and steal just like people who are not Christians. In many instances there is no difference in lifestyle choices than the people who do not believe in God.

In spite of the fact that we continue to sin, God still uses our vessels to do his work here on earth. Unfortunately many Christians are not available when God needs them to take on a mission that has divine implications. What happens next should bring shame upon many of us. Our God uses non-believers to carry out his Will. In most instances the non-believers are unaware that they are being used to fulfill God's Will. This is another mystery that God has included in his design to bring about the outcome that he so desires.

As you can see there are numerous ways in which God can use our Temples. Mature Christians have a better chance of lining up with God's Will by being conscious of when God is at work implementing his Will. By being conscious of God's hands at work, we have the opportunity to be available when God calls upon us for a divine mission. By the way, anything that God does is divine.

Let us all take another look at the purpose of our creation. It is to serve God at his pleasure. Keeping our Temples clean and being conscious and ready when God calls are some of the most important purposes of our creation. (Colossians 1:16, Revelation 4:11) Too many of us are not conscious and ready when God calls on us for a divine mission. The cares and distractions of the world are major strongholds that keep many of us unable to do God's Will at any given moment. It makes me wonder what happens when some people are praying. Do they pray for their own will to be done or do they pray for God's Will to be done? Prayer is a two way conversation with God. Although many people believe this, they do not practice it.

I know of people who spend hours praying to God but yet do not stop and listen to what He has to say. They present a long list of things that they want God to help them with but seldom take the time to listen to God's response. An important responsibility for a believer is to know God's voice and continually seek to hear from him. As we grow in maturity in our relationship with God, knowing his voice and responding to his direction can bring change to any situation. Our Temples can be used as the vessels that God uses to bring change to a given situation. Again this requires our ability to hear and recognize his voice.

At this point we must present another part of the mystery in our understanding of our purpose as vessels that God uses. We are God's sheep and should know his voice. (John 10:3-4) A reality that we must all deal with is that at any given time there may be one or more of three voices in our head. The first of these voices is our own voice. It is tempered with our own desires that may or may not line up with God's Will. The second voice that we may hear is Satan's voice. Be assured that he will lead you in a direction that is away from God's Will. The most important voice that we will hear is God's voice. He is continually communicating with us. Because of our relationship with him and God proving himself over and over again in our lives, we should know his voice.

The certainty of a relationship with God hinges on a two way conversation of prayer with him. This is an area of the church's teaching that is lacking and not emphasized enough. Our Temples are supposed to be in constant communication with God. God is always speaking to us. The problem is that we are not always listening when he is communicating with us. Temples therefore should also be listening posts for God to provide direction to his people and the world. Some Christians actually have the gift of prophesy while others hold the office of Prophet. In this capacity those who are chosen to speak messages from God are leaders that bring both warnings and blessings to God's people and the world. As you can see, God communicates with his human Temples and uses them to both warn and bless others.

THIS LIFE

It is a wonderful gift to experience this life. The ability to see with our eyes, to hear with our ears, to smell, to taste, to touch and feel the world around us took a brilliant mind to create our living experience. While it is true that billions of people have now experienced this life with the essence of their being in a vessel made of dirt, many still do not understand the purpose of our existence. History has left us many clues about where we came from and where we will end up. Ignoring this knowledge and elevating man as the center of the universe has severely damaged our ability to experience the joy and purpose of our creation. Because our lives are brief when compared to eternity, it makes the task of understanding our purpose and meaning in life very important.

The mystery of life is revealed in the scriptures of the Bible. The Old and New Testaments provide insight into how we should experience this life. When we fail to learn from the mistakes of the past which are revealed in the Old and New Testaments, the joy of living cannot be fully realized. As we continue living and ignore the principles of the New Testament, our lives take a journey that will not lead to the love, joy, peace and happiness that was originally intended for us. There is a simple explanation for this. An essential element of our existence is missing from many people's lives. It is the constant relationship and communion with God, the creator of all.

It is God's intelligent design that has created us all. He is responsible for the environment that we exist in as well as the natural and spiritual laws that govern our lives. Without God as our necessary being, we dependent beings cannot exist and have meaning and purpose. Many people try to live independently from him and the result is the present condition of the world. There is no world peace. There is a lack of compassion and tolerance for others. Violence is a major tool used for change and control of others. There is so much corruption and demonic influence on mankind that many people cannot distinguish between right and wrong or good and evil. All of this because people will not follow the roadmap that God has given us, the Bible.

The Bible tells us the purpose of our creation. It chronicles the spirit war and the spiritual battles that we all must live through. Once we embrace God's purpose for our lives, we can have a meaningful existence as well as experience the peace, joy and happiness that he originally intended for us. This life, our bodies and this environment were designed for us to conduct ourselves in a certain way. When we begin to violate the natural and spiritual principles that God has ordained, we begin to experience the effects of our actions. These violations fall into the category of what we call sin. Sin is simply a violation of God's boundaries for our lives.

God gives us free will that allows us to violate these boundaries. When we violate these boundaries, we damage our relationship with him. The problem then becomes how do we restore our relationship with God after violating these boundaries? This is the whole point of Christianity. God knows that we will violate his boundaries for our lives. It is critical to know whether we violate these boundaries intentionally or unintentionally. Willful violations are much more difficult to deal with than unintentional ones. Because God is so great, he included a plan for restoring our relationship with him for both types of sin. His answer is Jesus. It takes a relationship with Jesus to have the ability to restore fellowship and relationship with God. It cannot be done any other way. With the natural and spiritual laws that are in place, only a transcendent God could repair the damage caused by sin. It is beyond our natural and spiritual abilities to do so.

Following the Bible as our roadmap keeps us in tune with the Will of God. The Will of God is something that the world in its natural state cannot understand. The world cannot perceive of the things of God and is in conflict with his Will. This is not something that is new to Christianity. Rebellion against God has always been at the center of man's struggle to understand the purpose of his creation. Changing God's original design to gain control of others, the environment and the natural resources that are supposed to sustain us all carries consequences. When God created the earth, he provided enough resources for everyone to live well. Man's selfish nature has caused so much suffering for God's people as well as the rest of the world. This spirit of control is at the heart of the spiritual war. What can God's people do about this? That is a good question.

The purpose of our creation now comes into focus. We are all spiritual beings on a human adventure. God created us to experience a loving relationship with him and our brothers and sisters in Christ. For some reason not revealed to us, angels do not have the same ability or opportunity to experience life in a human body. Our bodies were specially designed for us to experience the emotions of love, joy, peace and happiness. We were created in God's image. Theologians believe and teach that we are in the middle of a spiritual war. Because we are human, we have the limitations of being in a body that is not eternal. The other beings that are involved in this spiritual war are eternal. They can and do use us to fight against the opposing forces. When we sin, we support Satan and his fight against God. Unfortunately, Satan has a vast number of human supporters. Looking at the condition of the world and how people act, it seems as though Satan is winning the war in sheer numbers.

Numbers can be deceiving. Satan may have the numbers but God has already won the war. Satan knows that he has already been defeated. He wants to corrupt and influence as many people as he can to join him when he is finally punished for his rebellion against God. An important purpose for every Christian is to win souls, bringing as many people as possible into God's kingdom. This is not an easy task. The church is supposed to be the vehicle to accomplish this on a large scale but it has also been infiltrated and corrupted by Satan and his followers. When we look at the church today, there are so many violations of God's laws it is difficult to imagine how it can ever be effective in the spirit war. It is now up to individual Christians to maintain God's standards and bring these standards back to God's church. Many church leaders have fallen prey to the corruption of the money and power that the church attracts. We see many church leaders who do not have a humble servant's heart

Today we see millionaire Pastors with body guards, several mansions and more money than many towns or cities. Satan has corrupted many church leaders and a lot of them do not even know it. It will be the humble Christian with a servant's heart that will bring God's church back to its original purpose. In the meantime, the spirit war continues at an accelerated pace. Knowing our purpose in creation and knowing God's will is an essential weapon in the spirit war. Our relationship with Jesus keeps our minds and bodies in step with God's will. The vessels that God has given us to live our lives in are designed to be Temples. We should treat them as such and allow God to use us in the spirit war.

We are God's Temple keepers. It is a shame when God's own Temples are used against him in the spirit war. As I stated earlier, our lifestyles and actions determine which side of the spirit war we support. Not reading and knowing our Bible leaves us vulnerable to the world system and its influences. This together with not having a good relationship with Jesus sets us up for failure. The world system has so de-sensitized us that we cannot see corruption and evil for what it is. When we are in the habit of lining up every situation that confronts us in this life with the word of God, it clearly reveals to us what is right or wrong, good or evil in every situation. It is every Christian's responsibility to recognize which actions cause us to make our Temples unclean.

In the beginning this was not a concern. We were clean before God until the fall of Adam and Eve. Our relationship with God was holy in nature and free of the sin that separates us from him. Since the fall of mankind and the damage that it has caused to our relationship with God, it has been a battle with the world system to keep our Temples clean. The mission of the world system with Satan as its leader is to keep our Temples (Bodies) in a state that is not holy before God. Unfortunately for many Christians, this is a normal state of being. For many others, it is a constant struggle to fight off the influences of Satan and the world system.

When Satan and his follows distract and influence our lives, we are not ready or available for God to use in his fight against the dark forces in the spirit war. Our original purpose in God's creation is to have a loving relationship with him. This is hindered by our relationship with the desires of the world and its rebellion against

God. It is a cycle that continually repeats itself. The more that we are involved with the world system and its rebellion against God, the more restoration we need in our relationship with him. Our purpose and meaning especially in the spirit war becomes ineffective.

One of the most important things that we can do is to keep our Temples (Bodies) clean and ready for God to use. Some of us will be on the front lines of the spirit war while others will teach, preach and uphold kingdom values. Many will use their spiritual gifts to bring blessings and healing to many. Understanding and following God's roadmap in the Bible can ensure that we are in God's will and ready to be used by him when he decides to project his Will. Ultimately our purpose in creation is to serve God. We must do it in a manner that glorifies him while honoring the Temples that he has given to us. Once we have completed our mission on earth, the Lord will call us home. At this point we have graduated to heaven

The death of one of God's Temples is a time of celebration. The release of an eternal soul is an example for all who still remain alive. It is a reminder to all that we too have the same future. It is too late to make adjustments for the one who has already been released by the death of the Temple. Acknowledging this death allows everyone that was involved in this person's life a chance to make adjustments to their lives to ensure a joyful eternity.

Funerals are for the living but many people miss this point. They are a warning that all will experience the transition into eternity. True Christians have an advantage in this transition because of our relationship with the Holy Spirit that dwells in all of us. The Holy Spirit is the guarantee that Christ has already paid the price for all sins committed in the body (Temple) so that no judgment for eternal separation from God will take place.

The scripture reveals that there are many rewards for those who honor and keep their Temples clean. God honors and blesses those who put their faith in his son Jesus. By honoring him with keeping his commandments and keeping our Temples clean, we are sure to graduate to heaven.

A concept that is misunderstood by most people is their desire to get into heaven. They have it backwards. Instead of trying to live a life with heaven as your final destination, we should all live our lives trying to get heaven into us. If we are in the habit of heaven, when we die it will be a much easier transition. It will be like taking our clothes off when we are finished with them. Our bodies will no longer be necessary.

Think about it. If we now enjoy all the perversions and sins of this world, we will not want to experience the joy, peace and happiness of heaven. The saints praising, thanking, loving and the fellowship with God will not be exciting enough for people who enjoy the perversions of this world. The desires of the flesh will still remain in their hearts.

Heaven will be a place of peace, joy and laughter of the soul. No tears. There will be no people who tell lies or who want to do harm to others. No more greed and selfishness. We will be eternally separated from those who rejected our Lord and Savior Jesus Christ. Evil will be destroyed. Death and pain will no longer exist. There will be no more temptations. All sins are paid for by the blood of Jesus so no debt for sin will exist. Love will be the center of our existence. God will be our all in all. Why would anyone not want to be a part of this?

It is necessary to address all those who reject God's free gift of salvation. The scriptures are clear. God desires that everyone be saved. (1Timothy: 2:4) In the book of Romans the apostle Paul tells us firmly that anyone who calls on the name of the Lord will be saved. The process is spelled out for anyone who wants to graduate to heaven. (Romans 10:9-13). When the Lord comes to judge the living and the dead, there will be no excuse for those who rejected his lordship and free gift of salvation.

Jesus stated many times during his ministry that the kingdom of God was at hand. This is still an invitation to all who are willing to forsake sin and the desires of the flesh. Honoring God by keeping our Temples clean is a good start for our journey to and final destination, heaven. Living a clean (holy) life is a requirement that cannot be waived. God requires holiness from us in order to be in a relationship with him. There is only one way for us to be holy and that is to take on the righteousness of Christ. Without it, we cannot see or enter into the kingdom of heaven.

FREEDOM AND ACCOUNTABILITY

All of us must accept the fact that we are spiritual beings living in human bodies that will eventually die. If the death of our body is the end of life, that is one thing. There is enough evidence however that shows that life goes on after death and we need to prepare for it. Some studies have been documented that reveal a common experience shared by people who have had a near death experience (NDE). Author Michael Talbot in his book entitled "The Holographic Universe" expands on the results of these studies as well as studies on people who have had out of body experiences (OBE). A common experience shared by people who have had a NDE is the life review during the death process. Those who were conscious enough to remember what they went through during their time near death speak of seeing their whole life flashing before them. It is a phenomenon in which they could see everything that happened during their lifetime presented to them at a very fast pace. It was fast but they had enough time to see their lives from the beginning to the end.

During the life review they could experience various emotions. Included in these emotions were, love, hate, regret, fear etc. When it came to the wrong things that they had done in their lives, they had an overwhelming feeling of sorrow. When they experienced a happy moment during the life review, it brought emotions of joy. All of this occurred in a matter of seconds.

Another part of this life review was experiencing the beings of light that were present while all of this was taking place. This is where the NDE experience presented in the book "The Holographic Universe" differs greatly from the doctrine of death in the Bible. According to the accounts in the book "The Holographic Universe", the vast majority of people who could remember their NDE said that the beings of light did not judge them. There were no universal feelings of condemnation. Heaven and Hell were not a part of this experience. There were two basic concerns about the choices that they made in their lives. Did they do it with love and did they learn something from their choices? The only difference for them and the people who would not be brought back to life is that they were given another chance to do things right.

The NDE is a phenomenon that has been recorded and verified in a scientific manner. Although this experience is real to those who have experienced it, it goes against the Bible's doctrine of the after-life experience. Because of the Gospel of Jesus Christ and his resurrection, we Christians must have faith in him and believe in his account of the reality of death over those who only experienced death for a few moments.

Another important point that should be made is that many of the people who shared this experience were not very spiritually minded before the life review. After going through the life review process and returning to this life, these people were a lot more loving, caring and overall more spiritually minded. In other words, they cared about how their actions affected others. People who are more spiritually minded tend to have what is referred to as a "servant's heart". This is directly related to the message and teachings of Jesus. Having a servant's heart entails being concerned about the welfare of others. It also entails helping others by sharing eternal spiritual truths such as the Gospel of Jesus Christ and being accountable for not doing what is right in the eyes of God.

The freedom to live without any restrictions or accountability may seem good but taking the welfare of others into account puts a different light on this freedom. It has always been difficult to understand why some people can do the evil things that they do. There are two explanations that may shed some light on understanding the phenomenon of evil. First, there is the belief that there is no objective morality. Second, there is no accountability for actions that hurt others and yourself.

Let us take a look at the concept of objective morality. Atheists believe that morality is a process of development over time in human existence. There are different standards of morality depending on your socialization in this world. This explains how some people who live in certain environments can develop destructive behaviors. It becomes even more destructive when the people who are in authority support and promote this kind of behavior. We have seen over the course of history the rise and fall of many civilizations because of this. The world has witnessed atrocities, racism, discrimination and certain cultures and races wanting to dominate their countries and even the world. The common thread that ties all of these things together is evil. Evil is a spiritual condition that allows people to act in a selfish destructive way. It is one thing to hurt ones' self but to inflict harm upon others takes evil to a whole new level.

The spiritual environment that causes and supports evil to exist has three sources that can be readily identified. The first is a supernatural being named Satan and the second is the God given right to choose right or wrong. The third source which can be extremely destructive is the desires of the flesh (our sinful nature). Doing what is right is a choice that on the surface seems easy. Living in this world of relative values and moralities has proven more difficult than most people can imagine. In fact, doing what is right in many instances takes a lot more time and effort than doing what is wrong. Doing evil on the other hand has proven to be much easier for the majority of people in this world. The question now becomes, why do some people choose to do evil? The simple answer is that they do not believe in or recognize that there is such a thing as objective morality. Everything that they believe in is subjective or related to those in authority over them. If the society or environment that they live in promotes a lack of objective morality, this will be their reality.

Living in a situation such as this leads to spiritual decay in which evil flourishes. Once it starts, it is very difficult to reverse the spiritual damage. It is like being a drug addict trying to get back to a normal state of being. After someone finds out that no matter how much of a drug they take, they will never feel as good as they did before they got high the first time. There is an emptiness that they are trying to fill that cannot be satisfied. There is only a spiritual solution to this situation.

When we talk about spiritual solutions and spiritual things, we must understand that there are objective spiritual truths as well as objective spiritual morality in behavior. We are all spiritual beings. Some of us are more enlightened than others. The more that we know about our spiritual reality, the closer we come to understanding the purpose and meaning of life. Because of this, it becomes much clearer to see and identify evil from an objective point of view. The best explanation for all of this is the knowledge of a moral lawgiver that is the creator of our existence. It is God and God only who can be the objective moral authority. What other reference can we live by that is eternal?

It is a relationship with God that allows us to at least know that there is objective morality. Trying to understand morality without God is always subject to those in authority who may or may not be moral beings. We cannot depend on humans to be objective in their moral behavior because those who practice evil do not fear being held accountable for their actions. If someone does not fear being held accountable for their actions, how do they determine what is right and what is wrong? To gain a better understanding of this we must examine more closely what it is to be a spiritual being.

When we acknowledge God as the creator of the universe and his moral law authority, we must accept our accountability to him. Once Jesus Christ was resurrected from the dead, our relationship with God changed drastically. The Holy Spirit was sent to us to inhabit our bodies as Temples. This change brought even more accountability for us. We still have the freedom to choose good or evil but now we are doing it as Temples of the living God. The Bible speaks about our responsibilities to keep our bodies (Temples) clean. There are several passages in the Bible that discuss that our bodies are no longer our own but belong to God. Jesus purchased them with his own blood. (1 Corinthians 6:19-20) The Bible goes on to say that anyone who defiles a Temple of God will be destroyed by God. (1 Corinthians 3:17) As you can see objective morality is very important. It must be God's morality that is the standard and not ours. Knowing God and his objective morality is every Christian's responsibility. Living it can be difficult at times. When we do this, we are keeping our Temples clean.

As born again Christians we live in a world of constant conflict. We must make daily choices that put us at odds with the world and fellow Christians. Did you ever stop to think why this is a continual struggle? It is because as followers of Christ, we must carry on the mission that Jesus started here on earth

Jesus said in Matthew 10:34-40,"Do not suppose that I have come to bring peace to the earth. I did not come to bring peace, but a sword. For I have come to turn a man against his father, a daughter against her mother, a daughter-in-law against her mother-in-law. A man's enemies will be the members of his own household. Anyone who loves his father or mother more than me is not worthy of me. Anyone who loves his son or daughter more than me is not worthy of me. And anyone who does not take his cross and follow me is not worthy of me. Whoever finds his life will lose it, and whoever loses his life for my sake will find it. He who receives you receives me, and he who receives me receives the one who sent me".

Jesus is telling us in this passage of scripture that anyone who does not follow him in righteousness and follows the ways of the world cannot be a true follower of his. We must make a clear decision to choose him and his ways over sin. He demands total loyalty. Not even your mother or father can stand in-between you and your relationship with God. This is extremely difficult for most people to grasp. Every day we are presented with choices to either do things that please God or things that please the world. The world is so evil and pervasive that most people do not realize that they are sinning when they do. In this context sin seems normal. If our standards are that of the world, then we are in constant opposition to God and his standards. This is a dilemma for most Christians. We try to balance having a good relationship with the world and at the same time have a good relationship with God.

We are commanded to do two things for God that will ensure that we are in his will. First we must love the Lord God with all our heart and with all our soul and with all our minds and with all of our strength. Second, love your neighbor as self. (Mark 12:30-31) Looking at this from a natural point of view, this seems simple. When we look at this from a spiritual point of view, we see that loving God takes more than just saying that we love him. We must follow his commandments and obey him in all that we say and do. Loving your neighbor as self is even more problematic. Yes, we are commanded to love our neighbor but we are not commanded to love his ways or beliefs if they are contrary to God and his word. We are to love the sinner but hate the sin that he or she is involved in. Many people have a lot of difficulty with this. It is a source of much confusion. This is why we are to study to know God's word and ways so that when we are presented with something that is contrary to his Will, we can choose God's point of view and be in his Will.

The world does a good job of confusing us with what is right and what is wrong. They use the term "relative" to cloud many people's judgment. "It's right for me but may not be right for you" is a commonly used term or saying. Or they may say it is wrong now but it will be ok in the future. This is the case when the homosexual lifestyle was once an abomination before God and now it is socially acceptable by the world and its' standards. What is being miscommunicated is the fact that God's standards are eternal. It is our understanding and practice of them that brings on the confusion. Man has always known the difference between right and wrong but chooses to do wrong. This can also be attributed to demonic influences. Very few people will admit to being or doing evil. They truly believe that they are just and right in the things that they say and do. What is tragic is that others follow them knowing that what they do is wrong and say nothing. Look at the history of the United States and the treatment of the Native American Indians and the Black Slaves. Even so-called Christians went along with the killing of millions of Native Americans and the cruel treatment and enslavement of millions of African Americans.

Today we still see a spirit of supremacy over people. Jesus said that Christians should have the testimony of being a fellow servant and brother and sister to other Christians. When we look at the Christian church today, we see very little that resembles the example that Jesus taught us. There is a lot of confusion, strife, jealousy, competition and greed in the church today. There is very little unity. Each denomination believes that they are the only ones who know the truth. What is not being taught to many Christians is to seek a personal relationship with the Lord. Instead many churches promote a relationship with the church or its' leaders instead of a relationship with the Lord. This is a great source of conflict and confusion in the Christian church today. God is relegated to a minor role in the church while church activities and missions are placed above having a personal relationship with him.

In the book of Revelation John is shown a vision of the end times. It is interesting that Jesus tells John to write letters to the seven churches and their leaders. Jesus states that he will hold them accountable for not following his commandments. Some of these churches are leading people in completely the wrong direction away from Jesus. The vision is a warning to all that even the churches at the end times will suffer corruption. The purpose of the vision is to restore holiness to the church and its' people. Although this is a prophetic view of the future, the seven churches are being warned of the consequences if they do not change their ways. For God, holiness is not an option. The same holds true for the seven churches and their leaders.

The conflict with the world will never end until the final judgment of God. Christians must be prepared to fight the good fight until the end. If Jesus did not come to make peace with the world, then how can we? Our mission is to win as many souls as possible before the Lord's judgment day. Each of us was created to perform a specific mission that no one else can do. Realizing this and seeking God's Will for our lives is a part of the mystery of creation. God could do it all alone but chooses imperfect beings like us to do his work in tandem with his holy angels.

To have a good worldview Christians must adapt a spiritual warfare motif of reality to understand more of the mystery of creation. God could have created a world without sin. Instead he chose to create a world that would allow people to choose sin if they so desired. The world that he created is populated with free willed beings that have the ability to resist his Will. As a result, conflicts arise. In the spirit war our actions either support God and his Will or his enemy Satan. When we sin it gives more power and influence to Satan and his followers. This is why we must be careful in everything that we say and do. Imagine, Christians supporting Satan. This is the warning in the book of Revelation that John is writing about. The churches and their leaders are not following God and his holy ways but following Satan and his rebellion against God. We all will be accountable to God for the deeds that we commit while in the body. (2 Corinthians 5:10)

THE LAW, POLITICS, ECONOMICS AND CHRISTIANS

Christians are faced daily with many challenges as we try to live in peace with the world. The moral decay in American society can be directly attributed to changes in the law, politics and economic conditions. The vast majority of Christians believe that when man's laws are in conflict with God's laws, we should follow God's laws. (Acts 5:29) We are to do this even if there is a price or punishment for non-compliance to man's laws. (Jeremiah 42:6) Although the New Testament clearly states, "Remind them to be subject to rulers and authorities, to obey, to be ready for every good work" in Titus 3:1, this is where we as Christians must demonstrate and honor God's commandments.

According to the teaching of the majority of Christian churches, abortion is wrong and a sin. This goes back to the original Ten Commandments, "You shall not murder". (Exodus 20:13) The law of the US has granted women the right to choose whether or not they can terminate a pregnancy for health reasons or for convenience. This is an area where man's laws are in conflict with God's laws. We also know that having pre-marital sex is also wrong and a sin but many Christians engage in it anyway. The problem lies in the corruption of the world entering into the lives of Christians. We are becoming more and more de-sensitized and integrating with the ways of the world.

Recently the Supreme Court ruled in favor of gay/lesbian rights and equal protection under the law for this lifestyle. This is clearly in conflict with God's law. The scriptures teach us that those who engage in homosexual activities will not see the kingdom of God. What are we as Christians to do? First, we are to remember that this and other moral corruption was prophesized by Jesus himself as a sign of the end times for mankind. It is a continuation of the spiritual war that must be fought until the end. Society continues to redefine right and wrong, good and evil daily. We must be prepared for this and not be shocked. What Jesus stated in Matthew 24 6-15 will come to pass. Jesus said," You will hear of wars and rumors of wars, but see to it that you are not alarmed. Such things must happen, but the end is still to come. Nation will rise against nation, and kingdom against kingdom. There will be famines and earthquakes in various places. All these are the beginning of birth pains. Then you will be handed over to be persecuted and put to death, and you will be hated by all nations because of me. At that time many will turn away from the faith and will betray and hate each other, and many false prophets will appear and deceive many people. Because of the increase of wickedness, the love of most will grow cold, but he who stands firm to the end will be saved. And this gospel of the kingdom will be preached in the whole world as a testimony to all nations, and then the end will come. So when you see standing in the holy place 'the abomination that causes desolation,' spoken of through the prophet Daniel, let the reader understand".

The US on its journey of decay in society has now redefined marriage. The way that the US has redefined marriage is not a part of God's original design. Remember, it was God who created and ordained marriage. It started back in the Garden of Eden. God put man and woman together as one flesh in marriage. Man and woman were designed and created by God to have a holy relationship in marriage. Genesis 2:21-24 tells us, "So the LORD God caused the man to fall into a deep sleep; and while he was sleeping, he took one of the man's ribs and closed up the place with flesh. Then the LORD God made a woman from the rib he had taken out of the man, and he brought her to the man. The man said, "This is now bone of my bones and flesh of my flesh; she shall be called 'woman, ' for she was taken out of man". For this reason a man will leave his father and mother and be united to his wife, and they will become one flesh".

Politics and man's laws are becoming more and more in conflict with God's laws and commandments. We have observed what organized religion has done in the past in terms of honoring and obeying God's laws. The treatment of Native American Indians was truly evil. The same can be said about the treatment of African Americans in America's history. Just like the crusades in Europe, many terrible things were done in the name of God by the church. Corruption has always been a part of the church. Man continues to redefine what God has already ordained as moral. Society continues to turn away from God's morality and embraces a morality that is only relevant to present day laws, politics and economics

The Catholic Church has a self- imposed moral dilemma because of its own doctrine regarding Priests. This is all unnecessary. Instead of dealing with this dilemma as God originally designed for our lives, Pope Benedict VIII in 1022 banned Priests from getting married because of economic concerns. He did not want sons of Priests inheriting church property. Because women were considered such unworthy creatures and did not inherit property, daughters of Priests were considered legitimate until Pope Gregory ordered all children of Priests to be illegitimate. Because the church has imposed an unnatural burden on its clergy, many of them have been and are currently involved in sexual sins. As a result we are seeing many cases of child sex crimes, Priests with children out of wedlock as well as Nuns having babies. We can trace all of these problems back to Pope Benedict's decree to stop the clergy from being married for economic reasons. When we follow church leaders who engage in corruption, we too become corrupt.

What should Christians do in response to this knowledge? Learn from it. As corruption infiltrates the church, it also infiltrates individual Temples (Our bodies). We start to become de-sensitized to wrong doing because there are traditions and doctrines that must be followed if we are to be a part of a particular Christian denomination. Today we find so many denominations within the Christian faith. Many of them are no longer Christ centered but have become man centered. Too many Christians follow church leaders who are moving away from God's laws for economic and political reasons. Churches are now big business. Whenever there is a lot of money and resources involved, corruption finds an open door.

The Old Testament shows examples of what happened to God's people when they chose to break his commandments. God expected exact obedience to his laws and the penalties for not obeying them were swift in most cases. Now that we have a high priest in Jesus to intercede on our behalf when we break God's laws, the punishment for our sins have been paid for by the cross of Jesus. Having a relationship with Jesus covers a multitude of sins. What is it that makes Christianity so unique in the world? The worst thing that can happen to us is death and then we go to Heaven.

A question that many Non-Christians ask is: why are there so many denominations and different churches in Christianity? The answer is that there are so many different standards, morals, traditions and values between churches. People want different things out of life. Not every Christian seeks to honor and please God. Many Christians have not been properly taught to live as Christ has commanded. As stated previously, manmade laws, economic conditions and politics have split many churches. Many church leaders interpret God's commandments to suit their own agendas. It would be so much easier if they all started with one simple standard. Keep your Temple clean so that the spirit of God will have a holy place to dwell. In this light manmade laws that are in conflict with God's laws could be handled easily. A Christian would know that by turning away from God's commandments, he or she would not be keeping their Temple clean.

A BETTER UNDERSTANDING

The mystery of creation, the mystery of the creator and his creature, the purpose and meaning of life are all fascinating topics of discussion. There is no discipline or scientific understanding that can bring clarity to this discussion except Christianity. To understand the concepts of good and evil, love, joy, jealousy, hate and other emotions, they must have a moral dimension to them. Without a moral lawgiver these feelings and emotions cannot be put into any kind of meaningful relationship with this life. Christianity deals with all of these issues and puts them all in proper prospective with an intelligent design and designer of these feelings and emotions.

Since mankind has broken its relationship with its creator, this lack of relationship has distorted the linkage of morals and values to an objective eternal source. God is the designer, creator and moral authority of creation. He is the only reference that we have to relate to creation and its purpose. Not knowing the mind of God and his gift of free will to human beings is also a great mystery. The right to choose right or wrong, good or evil without God as a reference is chaos. God so honors the right of free will that he is even willing to allow his creation to destroy itself. God desires that we choose his moral authority freely but does not compel anyone to do it against their free will. Looking at the condition of the world and the evil that people do, many people ask, "Why does God allow this to happen?"

Another question posed by many people is, "Where is God when bad things happen?" With the world in its present condition and evil all around us, many people question why he would allow evil to be so powerful. When we think of God's character and attributes, they are totally different from the world that he has created. God is an all-powerful, all-good and all-knowing God. Why would he create a world and let it be controlled by evil? Some people believe that God is not present in the world today even though he created it. Many unbelievers ask: "Where is God? Show him to us". Christians should be able to provide answers to these questions.

The Old Testament provides many accounts of when God was present and active in the lives of his people. He was present and dealt with evil on a regular basis. God was present before the creation of the known universe. This is just one part of his many attributes. Because he is an uncreated being, he is present all the time. He cannot help it. It is a part of his nature. God is everywhere. His presence is inside and outside the known universe. He has the ability to transcend our world when he so desires. The incarnation of Jesus Christ is the best example of God's ability to transcend our world. Jesus' interaction and influence on the world cannot be overstated. What he accomplished in his short time on earth was incredible. Christianity has the best explanation for understanding the purpose and the meaning of life. Jesus bridged the gap between mankind and their place in eternity. It is in having a relationship with Jesus the creator of life that makes this all possible. Christians are now in the best position to answer the question of, "Where is God?"

Because evil is so prevalent throughout history, dealing with it has always been a task for the church. Science, philosophy and other disciplines do not address evil adequately. Christianity deals with the problem of evil through a warfare motif. Evil is not a part of God's Will for his creation. It is a part of creation that exists because of the original design of the known universe. In order to know and experience love, the possibility of hate and rejection must also exist. Stated another way, a part of God's design included the concept of risk. God risked his free willed creatures choosing hate over love and evil over good. This is a self-imposed constraint that God put on himself. His Will and desire is for us to choose love and to do what is good according to his Will and purpose. Because of the spiritual warfare motif, there are evil spiritual beings that entice and influence humans to join them in their rebellion against God. When humans rebel against God's Will of love and doing what is right, sin and corruption separates us from God.

Because God loves us, a plan of redemption and restoration of relationship was put into place. A part of this restoration process with God includes certain actions (confession, repentance, baptism and the Lord's Supper). By taking these actions, they cleanse us of the sin and corruption that is acquired when rebelling against God and his righteousness. In return God provides his spiritual presence in the form of the Holy Spirit to live in the bodies of those who participate in these sacraments. This is the reason why Christians are in the best position to answer the question of, "Where is God?"

Restoring the relationship between God and mankind is a process that started with altars to the God of the Jews, God's chosen people. Once God called his people to be a unique nation separated from all others, a central center of worship was established. This central place of worship in the Old Testament is where the presence of God dwelled. This external place of worship was the primary way to come into God's presence. Once God established and ordained a meeting place for his people, only certain people were allowed to enter into God's holy meeting place. Moses and his brother Aaron were the first to be allowed to be in God's presence in this meeting place. Anyone that was not consecrated to God and tried to enter into his presence was killed by God. Later on God ordained a holy Priesthood to enter into his presence on behalf of the people.

Another mystery of the Christian faith is the transformation from a creator/creature relationship to a parent/child relationship. God is the parent and we Christians are his children. Out of respect, reverence and obedience, we are to keep our bodies (Temples) clean where God's presence dwells. It is only proper that we keep it clean to please him since it no longer belongs to us. He has given us a special eternal gift to inhabit us, the Holy Spirit.

How we live our lives has a direct effect on the condition and state of our Temples. If we allow any and everything that the world system implants into our lives, then we cannot claim to have a clean Temple for the spirit of God to dwell in. This is a major dilemma for most Christians. Living in the world system is extremely hard without some compromises. Some of these compromises cause our Temples to be defiled. Some of the things that cause our Temples to be defiled are: filthy language, sexual perversions, lying, cheating, general dishonesty and a host of other activities that can violate the clean standards that God has ordained for all Christians.

Christianity is a unique religion in that it has a Temple system that is unlike any other religion in the world. It is Christ centered. Christianity teaches and requires each believer to become a separate but co-dependent Temple working in unison as a church with other believers. It is an important responsibility for each believer to keep their Temple clean so that corruption does not enter into the collective body of the church. Living and integrating into the world system has caused many believers to become de-sensitized to the things that corrupt and make our Temples unclean. The main purpose of this book is to teach, remind and develop a devotion to keeping our Temples clean. The Bible teaches us that our bodies (Temples) are not our own. They were bought with a price and that price was the precious blood of Jesus. (1 Corinthians 6:19-20) This is a part of the great mystery that our Lord and Savior designed and planned. This supports the intelligent design argument for creation. It is in this intelligent design that we can find the purpose for our lives and a greater understanding of why living in this world can be so difficult for believers.

One of the promises that Jesus made was the gift of the Holy Spirit after his resurrection and ascension to heaven. The Holy Spirit is the power of God that keeps believers close to God. The indwelling of the Holy Spirit inside the bodies of believers is the beginning of the

New Testament Church. This sealed a new covenant with believers of the Gospel of Jesus Christ and God. As a result of the atoning work that Jesus did on the cross, the spirit of God can now dwell individually and simultaneously in the bodies of all believers. This started a new Temple system for all believers. Born again Christians are Temples of the living God. Because of this, it is every Christian's responsibility to keep his or her Temple clean so that the spirit of God can have a clean (holy) place to dwell in.

Annie Lennox a music superstar during an interview with TV Host Tavis Smiley, made some very compelling remarks on national TV. She stated that she was not very religious. This is not surprising when you hear her reasons for her statement. Lennox stated that more hatred, violence, bigotry, discrimination, sexism and murders have been done in the name of religion then you can imagine. Instead of caring what happens to fellow human beings, some religions actually mistreat people. They can stand by and watch someone be hungry, cold, sick and do nothing. They mistreat them because they do not believe in the same things or attend the same place of worship. Different denominations within the same religion are at odds with each other because of differences in doctrine. Every religion believes that they are right and all the others are wrong. A common theme in Christianity today is that it is Ok to reject, not love and care for other people because they do not have the same religious beliefs.

Lennox went on to say that music is a universal way that people can come together. It does not matter what race, color, culture or religious background that you come from. There is a spirit of unity that music promotes. You would think that religion would have these same properties but it does not. Today's organized religions are extremely divisive. They are the reason for wars, discrimination, sexual violence and murder. Religions are specialized, divisive and opposed to being a part of the whole universe. Lennox believes that religion is destroying the world. There are too many standards, values and beliefs that are in conflict to have peace on earth. For the very wealthy, money is their God. If anything gets in the way of making and keeping money, it becomes a problem that will have to be dealt with.

Love is supposed to be the highest level of existence in this life. How can anyone achieve this with the many different beliefs that people have? Religion by its nature is divisive. It forces people to live a certain way of life or be considered lost in the world. Even worse, it causes people with different beliefs to become enemies. Even Christianity does this to other belief systems. The common problem with all of these different belief systems is that men are in charge of them. Once a belief system turns into a way of life and people are obligated to following the leaders of an organization, this is where confusion can begin. Following the doctrine of an organization becomes central to a way of life. Again, these organizations are man centered.

It is possible however to put God as the center of a belief system. Before we can do that we must identify who he is. This book supports the belief that Jesus Christ is God. The choice to follow him is directly linked to his resurrection from the dead proving that he is God. It is Jesus' standards that are preeminent once we decide that he is truly God.

If we claim to be Christians then Jesus must be our God. The road map that he left us to follow cannot be followed only when it is easy or convenient for us. There is a divine reason why we should follow this road map and that is to keep our presence before God as clean as humanly possible. As we grow in the knowledge and grace of our Lord and Savior, the road map becomes vital to our everyday existence. The road map contains instructions that can lead us away from dangerous situations and keep us safe.

THE NEW TEMPLE SYSTEM

Most religions in the world have and believe in brick and mortar Temples. This type of structure is common among most religions. Christians however, know that as members of the New Testament Church, we are all individual Temples of the living God. This is just one of the unique characteristics of being a born again Christian. Christianity is one of the few religions in the world that has a part of its creator living inside the bodies of true believers. Some prefer to say, dwelling inside of true believers. This was all made possible by the resurrection of Jesus Christ proving that he is God having power over life and death. Jesus' promise to send us a Comforter (the Holy Spirit) was the fulfillment of this promise. Because the Holy Spirit dwells in the bodies of God's people, this makes them Temples of the living God. (John 14:15-17) The Holy Spirit is a part of the Trinity of persons that make up God. The Godhead consists of God the Father, Jesus the Son and the Holy Spirit which make up the three persons of God that act in unison of purpose. This is another element of Christianity that separates it from all other belief systems.

There is an amazing difference between the people of God in the Old Testament and the people of God in the New Testament. Because of the original sin in the Garden of Eden, man's relationship with God was damaged and had to be restored. This was not possible until the resurrection of Jesus Christ. This was the beginning of the New Testament Church. True Christians understand this but the world in general does not. Jesus' resurrection allowed a transformation of God's relationship with his creation man, to become a father/child relationship. This relationship now includes spiritual DNA and inheritance rights because of the indwelling of the Holy Spirit in the believers of Jesus Christ.

Let us take a look at what the Bible has to say on this matter. In Romans 8:9-17 the Bible reveals, "You, however, are controlled not by the sinful nature but by the Spirit, if the Spirit of God lives in you. And if anyone does not have the Spirit of Christ, he does not belong to Christ. But if Christ is in you, your body is dead because of sin, yet your spirit is alive because of righteousness. And if the Spirit of him who raised Jesus from the dead is living in you, he who raised Christ from the dead will also give life to your mortal bodies through his Spirit, who lives in you. Therefore, brothers, we have an obligation--but it is not to the sinful nature, to live according to it. For if you live according to the sinful nature, you will die; but if by the Spirit you put to death the misdeeds of the body you will live, because those who are led by the Spirit of God are sons of God, For you did not receive a spirit that makes you a slave again to fear, but you received the Spirit of sonship And by him we cry, "Abba," Father." The Spirit himself testifies with our spirit that we are God's children. Now if we are children, then we are heirs--heirs of God and co-heirs with Christ, if indeed we share in his sufferings in order that we may also share in his glory".

A critical component of this theology is that you must believe in the resurrection of Jesus Christ as God. If you do not believe in the resurrection, then the rest of Christianity makes no sense. If Jesus did not rise from the grave after a terrible death, then he cannot claim to be God and we do not have to believe in him. The proof that true Christians have about this is the reality of the Holy Spirit that dwells in all of us. At this point I must add the fact that it is a personal relationship with our creator that makes this all possible. In other words, how he deals with me may be quite different from the way that he may deal with someone else. It is a father/child relationship. God knows our abilities and limitations and deals with us accordingly. Some of us grow spiritually at incredible rates and some of us never really get pass the baby stage of our relationship with him.

Being born again is the vehicle that God uses to transform his people into a rightful relationship with him. The born again experience is not an option. All Christians must have this life changing experience. As a part of the born again experience, we are transformed into Temples of the living God. No one in the Old Testament had this ability or access to this life transforming experience. This is what prepares us to graduate and bypass death into life. The body will die for sure but your soul will live forever with God. It is the new birth experience that provides this awesome new reality.

Being a temple of the living God is a serious responsibility for every Christian. Because of our interactions with the world, it is easy for us to damage, defile and even keep our Temples in a constant state of filth. We will refer to this state of being as dirty or unclean. Let us first cover what constitutes having a dirty Temple. The Bible reveals many examples of people in the New Testament that did not keep their Temples clean. Many of these examples were by choice. In the book of 1 Corinthians 6:9-10 the Bible reads," do you not know that wrongdoers will not inherit the kingdom of God? Do not be deceived: Neither the sexually immoral nor idolaters nor adulterers nor men who have sex with men nor thieves nor the greedy nor drunkards nor slanderers nor swindlers will inherit the kingdom of God". The reason why this is so important is because how you live your life determines whether or not your Temple (Body) is clean.

1Corinthians chapter 3:16-17 elaborates on this more. It states, "Don't you know that you yourselves are God's temple and that God's Spirit dwells in your midst? If anyone destroys God's temple, God will destroy that person; for God's temple is sacred, and you together are that temple. The Bible continues with sexual immorality that makes the Temple dirty. It states in 1 Corinthians 6:15-20. "Do you not know that your bodies are members of Christ himself? Shall I then take the members of Christ and unite them with a prostitute? Never! Do you not know that he who unites himself with a prostitute is one with her in body? For it is said, "The two will become one flesh." But he who unites himself with the Lord is one with him in spirit. Flee from sexual immorality. All other sins a man commits are outside his body, but he who sins sexually sins against his own body. Do you not know that your body is a temple of the Holy Spirit, who is in you, whom you have received from God? You are not your own; you were bought at a price. Therefore honor God with your body".

Although the people in the Old Testament did not have the ability to become Temples, God still used examples of their behavior to demonstrate the unclean ways that mankind lived. It was so bad that God had to give Ten Commandments to his people to live by. These commandments were so basic for clean living but no one could live up to them. If you broke any one of these commandments, it was counted as you broke them all. (James 2:10) When we look at the Ten Commandments one by one, we can see that if the people of the Old Testament were Temples, they would be dirty Temples if they failed to obey just one commandment.

The Lord God is the creative intelligent designer that spoke the world into existence. His design plan was very specific but he allowed his creation to have free will and the ability to go against his wonderful plan. As the intelligent designer, God used his power of omnipotence to foresee that men would disobey him and damage their relationship with him. Because of this, God came up with a plan of restoration that would redeem mankind and restore the relationship with him. Jesus Christ is the sole solution for this plan of restoration.

How could Jesus Christ be the one to restore man and his relationship with God? First we must understand who Jesus is and then what role he had to play in the plan of redemption. We must now turn to one of the most complicated and controversial concepts in Christianity, the Trinity. The Trinity is where it all begins. Christian Theologians understand God as three persons in one. They are God the Father, God the Son and God the Holy Spirit. They are co-equal members of the Godhead that work together in unison. Jesus Christ is the person of the Godhead that took on the mission to unfold the plan of redemption for mankind. It involved being born in human form yet still remaining a member of the Trinity. As a part of the plan of restoring man's relationship with the Trinity, Jesus gave up his powers as a deity during most of his life. He used his life as an example of how to relate to God the Father and the Holy Spirit.

The design of the plan was for Jesus to live a sin free life and offer himself as a pure perfect sacrifice which no man had ever done before. Men offered many sacrifices and offerings to God but they did not satisfy the requirement for God's justice that the original sin caused. In the book of Hebrews chapter 10:1-18, the Bible explains that all the sacrifices that men made to God did not make God feel better because of the original sin. There were not enough animals on earth that could be sacrificed as offerings to God to satisfy his justice. This is what the Bible reveals. "The law is only a shadow of the good things that are coming, not the realities themselves. For this reason it can never, by the same sacrifices repeated endlessly year after year, make perfect those who draw near to worship. If it could, would they not have stopped being offered? For the worshipers would have been cleansed once for all, and would no longer have felt guilty for their sins. But those sacrifices are an annual reminder of sins, because it is impossible for the blood of bulls and goats to take away sins. Therefore, when Christ came into the world, he said: "Sacrifice and offering you did not desire, but a body you prepared for me; with burnt offerings and sin offerings you were not pleased. Then I said, 'Here I am, it is written about me in the scroll. I have come to do your will, O God.' " First he said, "Sacrifices and offerings, burnt offerings and sin offerings you did not desire, nor were you pleased with them" (although the law required them to be made). Then he said, "Here I am, I have come to do your will." He sets aside the first to establish the second. And by that will, we have been made holy through the sacrifice of the body of Jesus Christ once for all. Day after day every priest stands and performs his religious duties again and again. He offers the same sacrifices which can never take away sins. But when this priest had offered for all time one sacrifice for sins, he sat down at the right hand of God.

Since that time he waits for his enemies to be made his footstool, because by one sacrifice he has made perfect forever those who are being made holy. The Holy Spirit also testifies to us about this. First he says: "This is the covenant I will make with them after that time, says the Lord. I will put my laws in their hearts and I will write them on their minds." Then he adds: "Their sins and lawless acts I will remember no more." And where these have been forgiven, there is no longer any sacrifice for sin".

As a part of this plan of redemption, Jesus would die a horrible death and be brought back to life in three days according to the scriptures. This would prove that he is God because he has power over life and death. Once Jesus was resurrected, all authority in heaven and on earth was given to him by God the Father. (Matthew 28:18) The next part of the plan of redemption involved the Holy Spirit. Before Jesus was crucified he told his followers that if he did not die, God the Father would not send the Holy Spirit. Why is this so important? The Holy Spirit is the power and proof of the new birth experience. Being born again must include the Holy Spirit as a part of the process of redemption. Ephesians 1:13-14 states, "And you also were included in Christ when you heard the word of truth, the gospel of your salvation. Having believed, you were marked in him with a seal, the promised Holy Spirit who is a deposit guaranteeing our inheritance until the redemption of those who are God's possession to the praise of his glory".

Now that we have a better understanding of the importance of being born again, we can now put the pieces together and take a closer look at the concept of being Temples of the living God. Once we make a confession of faith (Romans chapter 10), the process of becoming a Temple of the living God begins. If we truly confess to God with a sincere heart, he will hear us and send the Holy Spirit to dwell in us (inhabit our bodies). God at this point has declared us righteous. This is a unique phenomenon that only happens to

Christians. This is a fulfillment of one of the promises of God. As this process continues a definite change will occur in the life of the person who made a true confession of faith to God. The next important step in this process is to repent of all your sins and be baptized in the name of Jesus Christ. Another important part of this process is to get involved in a New Testament Church that will provide education, support and guidance for new believers. Because God has declared you righteous, you have a clean Temple. Now you have the awesome responsibility of keeping it clean.

What can we do to keep our Temples clean? This is where the moral laws of God show the power and authority of God. As Christians, our mission is contrary to the way that the world works. It's not about us as the world teaches. Fame, success and accumulation of material wealth are not our goals. All of these things tend to damage and make our Temples unclean. We forget our purpose in God's design and are not ready when he calls us to action because of all the distractions of the world. The world wants you to worry about the material things in this life but Jesus tells us clearly in Matthew 6:25-34 what we are to do. Jesus says, "Therefore I tell you, do not worry about your life, what you will eat or drink; or about your body, what you will wear. Is not life more than food and the body more than clothes? Look at the birds of the air; they do not sow or reap or store away in barns, and yet your heavenly Father feeds them. Are you not much more valuable than they? Can any one of you by worrying add a single hour to your life?"

"And why do you worry about clothes? See how the flowers of the field grow. They do not labor or spin. Yet I tell you that not even Solomon in all his splendor was dressed like one of these. If that is how God clothes the grass of the field, which is here today and tomorrow is thrown into the fire, will he not much more clothe you, you of little faith? So do not worry, saying, 'What shall we eat?' or 'What shall we drink?' or 'What shall we wear?' For the pagans run after all these things, and your heavenly Father knows that you need them. But seek first his kingdom and his righteousness, and all these things will be given to you as well. Therefore do not worry about tomorrow, for tomorrow will worry about itself. Each day has enough trouble of its own".

Now that we have this as our foundation, these spiritual principles must be expanded into all areas of our lives. If we depend on God for everything in faith, the concept of keeping our Temples clean should become the norm and not the exception. Our Temples can be used by God to bring salvation and healing to many. How is this possible? Remember, the Holy Spirit dwells in the bodies of true believers. This is the same power that created the universe and Jesus Christ. It is also the same power that raised Jesus from the grave and conquered death. Imagine the power and ability to access the resources of heaven to collide with our earthly reality. Of course God can use a Temple that is not so clean to accomplish his Will. But is this something that you want to be responsible for because you are not available for God to use? Remember, your body is no longer yours. It was bought with a price, a very high price, the blood of Jesus. You are redeemed and reconciled to God. Why would you not want to keep his Temple clean?

THE NEW FOCUS

Did you ever wonder how God identifies his people in the dispensation of Grace? It is the indwelling of the Holy Spirit in each believer .This is the Temple System that God designed. When God looks at his creation, he can see those who belong to him immediately. The gift of the Holy Spirit is the fulfillment of the promise that Jesus made to all those who would follow and believe in him. Every believer in the New Testament Church is an individual Temple for the spirit of God to inhabit. This is the guarantee that God made to us for our salvation. It is imperative to make the following statement now. Everything hinges on the resurrection of Jesus Christ. If Jesus was not raised from the dead, do not believe anything that is written or spoken about him. The indwelling of the Holy Spirit is the confirmation that the new birth experience has occurred. This is a part of God's plan to restore mankind to a relationship with him.

It is painfully obvious that all of us must die one day. Some belief systems teach that you will take on another life form or evolve into something else. Still others believe that when we die there is nothing after death. There is no agreement on this matter. What I find interesting is that people will buy insurance here on earth for events that may or may not happen. Knowing that we are all going to die, why would anyone not look into or get insurance for life after death if it is available?

The resurrection of Jesus Christ proving that he is God should compel us to believe that there is life after death. Look at the movement that was started that has impacted the whole world because of his resurrection. The disciples that were with Jesus were willing to die for their belief in the resurrection. They actually saw the risen Christ and were willing to give their lives rather than deny the truth of Jesus' resurrection.

Jesus is the only person to be killed, experience death for three days as prophesied in the scriptures and rise to life again proving that he is God. The Bible gives a detailed account of what happened when Jesus died. The power of his resurrection dwarfs any human understanding of who he is. We must now take him by faith because our understanding of his power beyond the grave proves that he is God. He made promises to us all about life after death. One of the many attributes of God is that he cannot lie. After his resurrection Jesus declared, all authority in Heaven and Earth was given to him. (Mathew 28:18) Following Jesus now becomes an important choice for all of us.

If Jesus is truly God and he said there is no other life after death except through him, what will you do? I don't know about you but I am getting my insurance for life after death. You may even call it fire insurance if you like. Why fire insurance? Our salvation in Jesus protects us from a place called hell in which all who go there will burn forever. Jesus himself went down to hell and took the keys from Satan so that he controls who will spend eternity there. If Jesus is the only way out of hell, why not seek him to provide the assurance that you will not have to go there after death? I thank him every day for the fire insurance that he provides me and all other believers.

Jesus has done his part to redeem us. It is up to us to plan and prepare for the future? This cannot be a short term plan. This plan is going to be for all of eternity. The Bible teaches us that there is only one way and that way is Jesus. He requires us to be holy and sanctified. We must be born again of water and spirit. (John 3:5) We are required to join in fellowship with other believers to worship him and to encourage and support each other. Christians must separate themselves from non-believers and maintain the standards that God has ordained for our lives.

The world system is moving closer and closer to the lifestyles that God warned us against. It will be a challenge for most Christians not to integrate and accept the values of the world system. Every day we are asked to lower God's standards and join the world system and support Satan and his ways. We cannot serve two masters so we will have to make some hard choices. For some of us, not joining the world system will cause much suffering. For others, it might even mean death. All of these things are discussed in the Bible. None of this should be a surprise to anyone who is a true Christian. Unfortunately many Christians suffer from amnesia.

The Bible has an answer for most of life's issues. You may not like the answer, but it is there for you to discover. Discovering eternal spiritual truths is a part of our Christian journey. One phenomenon that comes to mind is that every Sunday Christians all over the world come together to praise and worship God. They all learn about him and his character. They claim Jesus Christ is Lord. They commit to following him. When they leave church on that Sunday and start the rest of their week, it is as if they did not hear a word that was preached that Sunday. The vast majority of Christians go back to their old ways. Some Christians share some of the same values and beliefs as non-believers.

What can we say about this? Again we must turn to the Bible and one of the parables that Jesus used to teach a large crowd of people. In the book of Matthew chapter 13 verses 1-9 the Bible teaches the following: "That same day Jesus went out of the house and sat by the lake. Such large crowds gathered around him that he got into a boat and sat in it while all the people stood on the shore. Then he told them many things in parables, saying: "A farmer went out to sow his seed. As he was scattering the seed, some fell along the path, and the birds came and ate it up. Some fell on rocky places, where it did not have much soil. It sprang up quickly, because the soil was shallow. But when the sun came up, the plants were scorched, and they withered because they had no root. Other seed fell among thorns, which grew up and choked the plants. Still other seed fell on good soil, where it produced a crop a hundred, sixty or thirty times what was sown. He who has ears, let him hear".

Christians are victims of this process. They go to church, hear the Word of God and within hours forget everything that they heard and learned. This is consistent with what Jesus said about the vast number of people who will be lost and the small number of people who will be saved. It is Satan's mission to distract us and to keep us from remembering who we are in Christ. How can we make disciples of all nations if our priorities line up with Satan and his world? Temptations are many and some are great. Whatever you have a weakness for in this world Satan and his followers will use it against you. The primary weapon that he uses is described in the parable of the sower of the seeds. It all involves our ability to keep and practice what we learn from our spiritual leaders, brothers and sisters in Christ and the Holy Spirit.

It is said that Sunday is the most segregated day of the week. Christians are supposed to be one body serving Christ. Every Sunday similar messages are spoken to congregations all over the world. There are so many divisions and denominations with Christianity, who can really say that they know God's Will? One group emphasizes certain parts of the Bible while others emphasize other parts. No one has a complete picture so what are we to do?

Society's change their values and laws to be more inclusive of different lifestyles. As a result, many of them no longer line up with the word of God. People go to church on Sunday to learn God's Will for clean living and yet during the rest of the week, they are living in peace with the world and its wicked ways. The Bible is clear in that you cannot serve two masters (Luke 16:13, Matthew 6:24). This is where a lot of Christians get into trouble. They believe that they can have it all. Serving God and then serving his enemy the world is normal for a lot of people. Since Satan is the ruler of this world, those who choose to live by sinning against God are serving Satan. It has been stated many times that there is no neutrality in the spirit war. You must choose freely to serve God or by default you serve Satan.

Trying to serve two masters causes people to have a psychological condition that is very similar to amnesia. Christians lose their identity and are able to function in Satan's world but yet on occasion remember that they made a commitment to Christ. This is the dilemma for a lot of Christians. Serving two maters will definitely cause you to lose your identity as a child of God. This is a classic case of Christian amnesia.

There are several governments in this world that are promoting the values and morals of Sidon and Gomorrah. In Washington D.C., many decisions are being made that support Satan and his war with God. Growing up in America we were taught that the U.S. was founded on Christian values. When we look at the history of the U.S., there is very little evidence for this belief. There has always been white supremacy, the murder of Native Americans and the horrific treatment of African Americans by those in charge of this country. Today we see the government supporting everything except Christianity.

It should be no surprise that many Christians are living with one foot in the world while trying to live a Godly life. This is where more trouble begins. Today's Christians want to live in peace with the world. What most Christians do not understand is that the world does not want to live in peace with them. Christians are persecuted all over the world. This is the reality of the spiritual war. Since its inception, Christianity has not enjoyed a peaceful co-existence with the world. The spirit war is about souls. The question now becomes, how many souls will Satan take with him and how many souls will be saved by God?

As Christians, we are supposed to depend on God for everything. Many of us forget this and turn to Satan's world first to meet our needs. As a result we have been conditioned to seek the world's solutions to our problems rather than taking them to God. It is this process that hurts us more than anything else. If we go to God first for solutions to our problems, he will direct us to the best resolutions for our situations. He has blessed many people with gifts that can help us and he does use them to do so. The problems arise when we trust the world and its ways before we go to God for help. This conditioning has many people confused. Instead of seeking God's will in their lives, they trust the world to make the best decisions for them.

Every Christian's mission should be to seek God's Will in every situation that they find themselves in. Staying focused on the primary mission that God has assigned to every Christian is made difficult by the world. The world does not want us to keep our focus on God. We are constantly being seduced by the charms of the world which lead us to sin. The primary temptations that the world uses to corrupt most Christians are the love of money, power, corruption and the sexual lusts of the flesh. How do we resist this? First, trying to live in peace with the world is not the answer. We are at war with the world. Our focus must be to win souls. If we are not winning souls for Jesus, then we are not performing one of our primary missions. None of us can stay here in this world forever. The focus must be on our eternal destiny. Do we love the world or do we love Christ? How we live our lives determines who we really support and serve.

Presenting people with the Gospel of Jesus Christ is one of our most important commandments as Christians. When we fail to do this, it may result in someone being lost to the world. On that great day when Jesus judges the living and the dead, there will be no excuses for not accepting the free gift of salvation that was offered during our lifetimes on earth. Christians must present the Gospel. If it is rejected by those people who deny Christ, we have done our part. We are no longer responsible for someone's choice to reject Christ. They will stand before him condemned. (John 3:18) That person will not be able to say that they were never told or they did not know that there is a God that is going to hold them accountable for all their actions while they were alive.

No one wants to believe that they are serving Satan. The allure of money and power is so powerful that it seduces even the most devout Christian. Sexual perversions are even more devastating for most people. The Bible states that most people sin with their bodies.1 Corinthian 6:18 states, "Flee from sexual immorality. All other sins a man commits are outside his body, but he who sins sexually sins against his own body". The majority of people cannot resist sin because it feels so good. Corruption is a natural consequence of sin. It begins to permeate into every part of one's life. It is a powerful spirit that becomes so strong that it is almost impossible to resist. By the time that most people realize what has happened to them, it is extremely difficult to stop and repent. Satan uses the tools of shame, disgrace and fear to keep people in a state of sin and bondage. The person believes that people and especially God will never forgive them for what they have done. In this state of mind a person believes that they cannot be saved and surrenders the rest of their lives to Satan and his world.

Again, the focus must be on our eternal destiny. If we take our eyes off of Jesus for one second, we can be seduced and deceived by Satan and his world. We are to continually be prepared to fight Satan and his kingdom of darkness. There are no innocent by-standers. Either you choose to serve God or you are automatically serving Satan. Today you must decide which side of the spiritual war you will be on. The war is coming to an end. Where will you spend eternity? Will it be with God in his glory or with Satan in hell?

THE INTELLIGENT DESIGNER AND GRACE

Now that we have a better understanding of God's plan of redemption for mankind, we must take a closer look at God's original design plan. In fact, it is a question of design that brings clarity to every Christian's existence. There are some things that modern science will never be able to explain. The reason for this is because science cannot measure or understand everything. It has built in limitations that only deal with certain aspects of reality. Modern science fails miserably when trying to answer questions such as: what is the purpose of life? Why do I exist or why am I here? These questions require a different understanding of reality. When we discuss issues that deal with morality, hope, joy, love, peace, happiness, fear and most importantly evil, science is of very little value. Yes science can observe these traits of the human condition but science fails miserably in restoring these states of being to a healthy balance. This is due to the fact that science does not address the spiritual component of reality that directly impacts these states of being.

Let us take a look at evil for example. Why does evil exist? The world is waiting for science to provide a good explanation for the existence of evil. To date, all science can come up with are observations of evil. A major scientific breakthrough would be to isolate the origin of evil or find a systematic way of dealing with it like all other threats or diseases that threaten our human existence. Pure science can never achieve a solution to cure evil because science does not include all the elements of our human existence. It is the spiritual component of reality that is missing from scientific investigation. The spiritual component is one of the most important elements of our human existence.

Science has historical data on evil that dates back to the beginning of recorded writing. You would think by now a solution or cure would be forthcoming. Evil is a unique part of our human existence. Evil is protected and encouraged at all times by someone, something somewhere. It is so powerful that many people do not recognize that it is wrong. Evil by the world's standard falls into the category of relativity. What is evil to one person may not be evil to another. There is no universal standard for evil from a political, scientific, societal, cultural or national perspective. The only way to really deal with evil from an absolute perspective is morally via a spiritual perspective.

The Bible is the only true guide that we have to deal with issues like evil. Why the Bible? It deals with the origins of morality and provides us with a road map to deal with issues such as hope, fear, joy, love, peace, happiness and evil. The Bible is the only true authority that clearly identifies a linkage between these emotions and our experiences. The Bible is the authoritative source that describes the condition of our souls and how we relate to these emotions and experiences. It deals extensively with the relationship of our spirits to these emotions and experiences. Science, technology and even psychology are ever changing with new discoveries daily. Bible principles and spiritual laws have not changed since God ordained them.

This book supports the Intelligent Design argument for explaining the creation of the universe. It is impossible for something that does not exist to create something that does exist. In other words, something that exists cannot be created by something that does not exist. It follows that if something exists, someone or something caused it to exist. This is the case with the universe. It just did not happen on its own. Even the scientific explanation of the beginning of the universe has holes in it. If there was a Big Bang that started the universe, what caused the Big Bang? When we look at the complex attributes of the universe, its delicate balance and the ability to sustain life, it points to an intelligent design. From this we can conclude that if the universe does exist and it is of an intelligent design, there must be an Intelligent Designer (God). This Intelligent Designer left nothing to chance. It was all meticulously designed down to smallest element and detail. Natural and spiritual laws were created in the design for God's highest level creation, man. Morality, the knowledge of right and wrong are also parts of this design. Included in this design is a road map that if followed will lead to joy, peace, love and happiness for God's ultimate creation, man. Failure to follow this road map will result in evil flourishing, eternal pain, suffering and separation from the designer and creator of life, God.

The scientific explanation for the beginning of universe promotes the idea that the evolution of the universe happened by chance. All of reality just happened to come together to produce all that we know. According to modern science, the possibility of our human existence was left up to chance. Science believes that everything in the known universe lined up perfectly on its own to create and sustain life as we know it. Do you really believe that this is all due to chance in our vast universe? The intelligent design explanation for the creation of the universe explains the purpose for our lives. It identifies the person who is responsible for designing, implementing, completing and sustaining every phase of our existence.

There will always be opposing discussions on the beginning of the universe, the origin of mankind, and the purpose of life. There are just too many coincidences when it comes to God's involvement in the story of creation. From an intuitive perspective, something being created by nothing just does not make sense. The visible universe is a very intricate creation. When you look closely at it, it bares the signs of an extremely creative mind. If the universe exists, something or someone had to bring it in to being. Looking at the known universe and its vastness leads us to consider that there must be a greater power than the people living on earth.

No matter how advanced our society becomes there are objective spiritual truths that mankind must accept as boundaries of moral behavior. For the most part human nature is not good. When we look at history, the fact that when objective spiritual truths are not included in our decision making processes, evil in the world increases. The lack of morality and living in this world always provides a stage for conflict. Man's natural state of mind is to control others. He does this through fear, corruption, coercion, and even murder. This was never a part of God's original design. His design for us included living as brothers and sisters, loving one another, and caring about each other. What happened to change this?

All of this happened as a consequence of the original sin of Adam and Eve. When sin entered into God's creation, the entire universe went out of sync with God and suffered the same corruption. The safe natural environment that God created for mankind is no longer stable and subject to decay and corruption. Sin severed our relationship with God and he took his hand of protection away from us. As a result, we are at the mercy of natural disasters, manmade disasters as well as the demonic spirit world. Man cannot control these three forces. When we add in the dimensions of disease of the body and mental illness, it is obvious that we must be conscious of the necessity of being clean physically, emotionally and spiritually.

Free will and the freedom to choose our destinies are the vehicles that allowed corruption to enter into God's original design. The world was created without corruption for human beings to exist in. It is important to digress and discuss the concept of holiness at this time. In the beginning God created man to be holy. Because man was created holy, God could openly fellowship and have a good relationship with him. God's attribute of holiness requires that anyone in his presence be holy. Because God is omniscient he knew that man could choose sin over holiness. One of the mysteries of God is his willingness to let free will be corrupted. God does not want to force anyone to be holy if he or she does not want to. There is a price for not being holy. It is being eternally separated from God. There is a spirit of rebellion in many people. They do not want to believe that some of their free will choices will lead them to eternal separation from God and eternal punishment. Many people do not want to believe that they could spend eternity in a place called hell. There is another free will choice. You are free to believe in whatever you want to believe in. The lack of fear of a holy God does not change the objective spiritual truth about God and his justice.

The resurrection of Jesus Christ proved that he is God. He has power over life and death. Those who put their trust in him do not have to worry about the outcome when going through God's system of justice. Since Jesus holds the keys to both kingdoms of heaven and hell, it will be Jesus who decides who will be eternally punished in hell. Why should we believe there is a place called hell? When Jesus died, he descended into hell like all humans. Because he is God, death could not hold him (Acts: 2:24, 27) He preached to the people in hell and told them of things to come. (1 Peter 3:19)

Once sin entered the world through Adam and Eve, God put into motion a plan of redemption to restore his relationship with mankind. This plan was a very sophisticated plan to bring mankind back to God. It involved God himself, the moral boundaries that he created and a true system of justice for everyone. This system of justice has two elements. On one side of this system judgment and punishment is the final outcome. The other side of this system provides an advocate that prevents judgment and punishment. God's design plan for this part of his justice system is called grace. God provides an advocate to present petitions on our behalf that will ensure victory. The strict design parameter that must be adhered to in this plan is that there is one and only one advocate that can represent us. That advocate must be Jesus Christ. Since Jesus is God, he represents all who are guilty of sin before his father. Keep in mind that as God and judge, he has the power to guarantee victory in this justice system. If anyone goes through this system of justice without Jesus Christ as their advocate, they are sure to lose and face judgment and punishment. Why is it so important that Jesus represent us in this system of eternal justice? Christians are guaranteed a pardon because they put their faith and trusted Jesus to save them.

If you know anything about the Bible, Jesus Christ was a perfect sacrifice for the sins of the whole world. As God, Jesus paid the price for all sin past, present and future. Since he has already paid the price for our sins, if we reject him as our advocate in God's system of justice, we stand condemned of our sins and must be punished for them eternally. (John 3:18)

PROTECTING THE TEMPLE FROM SIN

There is an on-going effort to destroy God's Human Temple System. Because Christians are living Temples of God, today we see the spiritual war for souls intensifying. Sin is so prevalent in the world today that even the Christian church has fallen victim to its charms.

Because sin is woven into the fabric of everyday life, many of us have lost the ability to recognize it for what it is. It is the most devastating weapon that is used against God's people. It comes in so many different forms and combinations, even the most devout Christian can be seduced by its' charm.

Our bodies play a very important role in the spirit war. It can be used by both God and Satan. How we live our lives determine whether or not our bodies are being used for sinning (supporting Satan) or living holy (supporting God) Sin is the primary method that Satan uses to get people to support him. Why do so many people sin? Sin feels good. Unfortunately this is only true for a season and then it matures and brings death and destruction. God on the other hand wants you to keep your body holy because it is the Temple that his Holy Spirit dwells in. Remember, when we sin with our bodies, Satan can use us in the spirit war. By keeping our bodies holy, God's spirit can anoint and use us in the spirit war against Satan.

Let us consider some important points. First, some people choose to sin as a personal choice. Sins such as lying, cheating, stealing, adultery, greed, hatred of others, murder and a host of other human activities are included in this list. This list is certainly not exhaustive. Others are involved in sin because they have strongholds in their lives. Drug addictions, sexual perversions and fear are examples of strongholds that people experience in their lives. Personal choice sin and sin strongholds are two dimensions of the spirit war. Evil spiritual beings make up the most complicated part of the spiritual war.

When we put all three of these dimensions together, there must be a coherent strategy to deal with all of them. In the theological world the term "Deliverance Ministry" is widely used. This is an area in which many modern day churches fail to deal with adequately. Most Christian churches do not want to deal with this negative, fearful part of ministry. Many church leaders do not want to talk about Satan, hell or anything else that might remind people that there is a real spiritual war going on and their souls can be casualties of it.

Fortunately for many of us there are church leaders who truly preach and teach the whole council of God. They teach about the goodness of God but they also talk about the consequences of sin and our eternal destinies because of the deeds that we do while in our bodies. They provide a balanced approach to living a good clean life before God. All of us are subject to bad personal choices that lead to sin. Many of us are trapped by strongholds that are too powerful for us to escape on our own. When evil spiritual beings are added to the mix, we do not stand a chance without our Lord and Savior Jesus Christ.

Jesus provides a way for us to escape the consequences of sin through a relationship with him. He has already paid the price for all of our sins. By confessing our sins, repentance and proper administration of the sacraments, our personal sin choices and stronghold sins are forgiven in the eyes of God. Deliverance Ministry is a major tool that the church can use to aid us in maintaining a strong awareness of the spirit war through proper training. It provides a clear vision of the spirit war by the revelation of God's word given in scripture. A major part of Jesus' ministry was casting out evil spirits. If there is one area that the church needs to constantly train and teach, it is the role of evil spiritual beings.

The Catholic Church is leading the Christian world in resourcing and training its' leaders to deal with evil spiritual beings. Jesus demonstrated that the kingdom of God was at hand when the evil spirits of his day recognized him and were afraid of him. He demonstrated his love by casting out many demons from people and setting them free from demonic influences. As disciples of Jesus we too are supposed to carry on this important work and ministry. Let us take a closer look at some of the things that are involved in Deliverance Ministry.

There are spiritual laws that allow evil spiritual beings to have a place in a person's life. It begins with a free will choice. This is another part of the mystery of God that causes us to grow spiritually or hinders our ability to grow spiritually. A free will choice to sin whether intentionally or not has consequences that are both physical and spiritual. The act of choosing sin over God opens doors and gives evil spirits permission to enter and be in someone's life. With this access they can begin the process of demonization. Since Christians are living Temples and the property of God, we now have trespassers that have access to God's property when this occurs.

Yes. As Christians, we are Jesus' property. When we continue to choose sin and do not repent and seek God, an evil spirit's presence and influence can become stronger in our lives. At this point we have opened a door that allows that spirit to be in our lives. This door must be closed and the evil spirit evicted. The process of evicting evils spirits is called Deliverance. This is one area of ministry that many Christian denominations do not support. In fact, some Christian denominations do not want to even talk about it or recognize that Deliverance is an important ministry.

The concept of dealing with evil spirits should not come as a surprise to those of us who read the Bible and understand that this was an important part of Jesus' ministry. It should also not be a surprise to know that there are many different types of evil spirits, levels and powers associated with them. Something that is a little more challenging is the thought that a group of evil spirits can work together in unison to possess or demonize humans. A good illustration is the story of Jesus and his journey to the region of Gerasenses. In the book of Mark chapter 5 verses 1-20 the Bible reveals the following. "They went across the lake to the region of the Gerasenes. When Jesus got out of the boat, a man with an evil spirit came from the tombs to meet him. This man lived in the tombs, and no one could bind him anymore, not even with a chain. For he had often been chained hand and foot, but he tore the chains apart and broke the irons on his feet. No one was strong enough to subdue him. Night and day among the tombs and in the hills he would cry out and cut himself with stones. When he saw Jesus from a distance, he ran and fell on his knees in front of him. He shouted at the top of his voice, "What do you want with me, Jesus, Son of the Most High God? Swear to God that you won't torture me!" For Jesus had said to him, "Come out of this man, you evil spirit!" Then Jesus asked him, "What is your name?" "My name is Legion," he replied, "for we are many." And he begged Jesus again and again not to send them out of the area. A large herd of pigs was feeding on the nearby hillside the demons begged Jesus, "Send us among the pigs; allow us to go into them." He gave them permission, and the evil spirits came out and went into the pigs. The herd about two thousand in number, rushed down the steep bank into the lake and were drowned. Those tending the pigs ran off and reported this in the town and countryside, and the people went out to see what had happened. When they came to Jesus, they saw the man who had been possessed by the legion of demons, sitting there, dressed and in his right mind; and they were afraid. Those who had seen it told the people what had happened to the demon-possessed man--and told about the pigs as well. Then the people began to plead with Jesus to leave their region. As Jesus was getting into the boat, the man who had been demon-possessed begged to go with him. Jesus did not let him, but said, "Go home to your family and tell them how much the Lord has done for you, and how he has had mercy on you." So the man went away and began to tell in the Decapolis how much Jesus had done for him. And all the people were amazed."

This is the first reference of multiple spirits working together to possess a human being. The demons recognized Jesus immediately as the son of God. Our identity in Christ will also be revealed when demons and other evil spirits encounter us. It was through this encounter with the demons that Jesus' identity as a deity was truly revealed. Jesus has given us authority over evil spirits. Our problem is that when we engage in sin, we give up our authority over them. So how do we deal with them? Before answering this question, I would like to clarify a couple of points before we continue.

Do you believe that a Christian can be demon possessed? The answer is no. Possession implies ownership. A child of God cannot be possessed by Satan or any other being. Christians are redeemed by the blood of Christ which means that Jesus paid a price for us. He is our rightful owner. Christians are Jesus possessed. Many people confuse possession with demonization.

Do you believe that a Christians can be demonized? The Bible does not make a distinction between believers and non-believers in terms of being demonized. So both believers and non-believers can be demonized. Since Jesus Christ redeemed us with his blood (paid the price), he is our rightful owner. When Christians are demonized by evil spirits, these evil spirits are trespassing on the property of Jesus Christ.

The power and essence of Deliverance Ministry is to use the delegated authority of Jesus Christ the rightful owner of all Christians, to command and evict trespassing evil spirits. When commanded in the name of Jesus, evil spirits have no choice but to go. They may have to be told several times to go but eventually they will have to obey the commands in Jesus' name. Deliverance for Christians represents the eviction of trespassing spirits.

As Christians, we will always be confronted by the enemies of God. When situations arise that do not make sense and medical considerations have been ruled out, it is usually some type of attack from Satan or his followers. It is impossible to cover every area that Deliverance may be required but we will cover some of the common areas of attack.

If you come from a family background that does not know Jesus Christ, you are already prone to working for Satan and his followers. Keep in mind that if you do not choose God and his righteousness, by default you have chosen Satan.

Satan uses the distractions of this world that include the love of money, lust, envy, strife, fear, jealousy, the lack of forgiveness and other sins as strongholds against us. These kinds of distractions have also taken hold of the Christian Church. Satan will use whatever tool, device or distraction available to make us take our eyes off of Jesus.

How does Deliverance Ministry deliver both families and individuals from the attacks on God's people? We must have a continual renewal of our minds which is the transformation that God requires of us to use his spiritual weapons

What are these weapons?

Ephesians chapter10 verses14-18 in the New Testament discusses God's spiritual weapons. They are commonly referred to as the "Whole armor of God" Included in these weapons are: The girdle of truth, the breastplate of righteousness, the helmet of salvation, the shield of faith, the shod of our feet with the gospel of peace and wielding the sword of the spirit which is the word of God.

Additionally it is the constant renewing of our minds that transforms us to adjust to the attacks of Satan. (Romans 12:2) We must constantly read the Bible and get new revelations from God in order to prepare for the next attack. It is also vitally important to invoke the Blood of Christ, Prayer, Praise, Speaking the Word of God, the name of Jesus and Perseverance to complete our spiritual weaponry.

One of the most vulnerable areas of attack is the family. Satan has a mission to destroy the family structure. This is especially true in African American families and can be directly linked to slavery. The problem of male leadership and the absence of a father in the home are areas of great concern in Deliverance Ministry. Slavery is the primary cause of the destruction of the Afro-American family structure. It has taken many generations to restore this structure back to the way that God originally designed it to be.

God designed the church and the family to work in an ordained and natural order. What we see as normal in many churches and homes today is not supported biblically. Both institutions are dysfunctional. God does not empower or ordain things that are not in his design. If there is power in a non-God ordained situation, where does this power come from? Now we can see where spiritual conflicts originate.

Take marriage for example. If we have two different faiths or backgrounds living under the same roof, there are normally two different spirits living in that household. If a conscious decision is not made to choose one belief over the other, conflicts will continually arise. This is a situation that the Bible refers to as not being "evenly yoked". (2 Corinthians 6:14-18) This is a recipe for conflict and the reason that God holds the man responsible for being the spiritual leader of the household. If the man of the house is not serving God, this opens the door and gives Satan permission to attack the family. By the same token if the woman of the house does not serve God, then she opens the door and gives Satan permission to attack the family. Husbands and wives must work together as God originally designed the family to function using his power. This is the only way that families can stand against Satan

This is why it is so important for Christians not to marry non-Christians. God will honor most marriages but the ones that are not in line with his original design will have more attacks and problems than the God ordained ones.

An important point worth mentioning is that if you have peace in your life and you are not serving God, watch out. Satan already has you and there is no real reason for him to attack you.

A sad situation that is a common occurrence among Christians is when Christians stay as babes in Christ and never develop their potential in the kingdom of God. Satan is happy with this result. These people are like POWs (Prisoners of War) in the spirit war. They cannot really be used effectively by God because they have not matured in their gifts and knowledge to fight in the spirit war.

One of the incredible joys of being a born again Christian and Temple of the living God is the ability to access the resources of Heaven. This is an area that most Christians do not fully understand or experience. The power dimension of Christianity is a relational experience that we share with our creator. Jesus demonstrated that it was only possible to do the things that he was able to do was because he followed what he saw his father God do. All of the miracles, signs and wonders that accompanied his ministry were actualized by a relationship that kept him in tune with the Will of his father. Jesus' faith and understanding his identity as the child of the living God allowed him to access the resources of Heaven. We too have the ability to access these resources but our relationship with the world in many instances blocks our access to them.

I find it quite interesting when Christians panic and cry out to God for help as though God does not know their situation. As soon as a little trouble or a difficult situation arises, Christians panic as much as non-Christians. Why is this? Christians really do not have faith in the promises of God. Many do not understand what it means to be a child of God and joint heirs with Christ. God has given us his spirit. This is the same spirit that created the universe, incarnated Jesus Christ, raised Jesus from the dead and now lives in each believer. Since God has given us his spirit and the authority that comes with it, why do so many Christians live a defeated life? They cry out to God for help as though he does not know what is happening to them. Defeated Christians who are suffering from amnesia forget who they are in Jesus and the gift of the Holy Spirit that dwells inside of them. They expect God to stop what he is doing and fix their situation. They do not realize or remember that God has already provided a way for them to access the resources of Heaven through the Holy Spirit that lives in them. We have previously discussed what is important in our role in the spirit war. Now it is time to really zero in on the power dimension of Christianity.

We must try to limit the amount of distractions in our lives which are the primary weapons that Satan uses against us. Our families, jobs and other cares of this world keep our focus and attention off of Jesus. When this happens, we are too distracted to be used by God in the war. God may have a specific mission for us but Satan moves some distracters in our path to keep us busy when the call from God comes.

Our bodies which are the Temples of the living God must be kept clean. When we engage in sin, it is difficult if not impossible for God to anoint and use us in the war. Also, we must know when, where and how to use our spiritual weapons. And finally, we must understand the difference between offensive and defensive weapons. Do you know what spiritual weapons are available to Christians?

It begins with the constant renewing of our minds that transforms us to adjust to the attacks of Satan. (Romans 12:2)We must constantly read the Bible and get new revelations from God in order to prepare for the next attack. Remember, God already knows the future. He wants us to join him in his work. If we are not being too distracted, we can hear from God and make the proper adjustments to fight in the war. Spiritual weapons also include using the Full Armor of God: (Ephesians 6:14-18)

When these weapons are used in combination with praise, speaking the Word of God, the name of Jesus and perseverance, there is no greater power in the universe.

KEEPING THE TEMPLE CLEAN

Every Christian has been given a road map to navigate this world. The Bible has an answer and solution to most of life's problems. It is surprising how many of us do not reference or consult it. Some of us actually try to navigate through this life without it. The Bible identifies ninety percent of the land mines that have the potential to blow up and destroy our lives. More amazing is the fact that many Christians do not want to learn to use the Bible but depend on others to tell them what the Bible reveals.

After the reformation of the church, Christians no longer had to follow the church blindly. They could experience the power of God's word on their own. The reformation brought accountability to the church and its leaders. God's standards apply to everyone. This is true for Christians as well as non-Christians. The New Testament church also includes accountability for church leaders but enforcing accountability on these leaders when they sin can be complicated. In some cases it may have the impact of splitting or destroying a church.

Examples of the church disciplining members and not its leaders who fall into sin are well known. There seems to be two sets of justice when it comes to God's kingdom here on earth. This is not how God originally designed his church to operate. There are higher levels of accountability for church leaders than there are for normal church members. What does all of this have to do with keeping our Temples clean? Remember, we serve a God of justice and all sin must be paid for no matter who commits it. Because Jesus has already paid the price for all sin, his church leaders who are acting under his authority will be held to a much higher standard of accountability. The care that these church leaders take of their own Temples (Bodies), are examples for those who follow them.

In too many instances the road map that God designed for all his people to follow is changed to conceal the wickedness of men. Church leaders believe that they are fooling God when they hide the sin in their lives. Nothing can be further from the truth. Because church leaders have a higher level of accountability, their actions when they commit sin are magnified. When anyone sins, it opens the door for evil spirits to be involved in their life. Continuing in sinful activities gives evil spirits permission to be present in our lives. Church leaders are no exception to this. How can anyone have a clean Temple and constantly open the door and invite evil spirits to be in their lives?

Our responsibility and reasonable service to God is to honor him by keeping our Temples clean. When we fail to follow the road map that God designed for us, we are subject to falling into the traps that make our Temples dirty. Our relationship with God is based on our knowledge of him and our faithfulness to him. The more that we know, the more accountable we are to him for our actions.

The Gospel is being preached and is reaching all corners of the earth. It is every Christian's responsibility to present it to as many people as God allows. Once we present it, people have the right to reject it. God does not want to drag anyone to Heaven that does not want to go. In order to make it into Heaven, God has ordained certain standards. One of them is to keep the Temple that he has given to you and I clean. How we live our lives will determine whether or not it is clean.

There are some who believe and teach that God is a loving God and would not punish evil disobedient people. Nothing could be more false. God's original design included a component of holiness for his creation. History has taught us that there are forces that are battling anything that is holy. Do not be surprised to find yourself at odds with the world if you are trying to live a holy life. This is the natural order of the spirit world. A spiritual war is being waged against anyone or anything that represents holiness. There is no neutrality in this war. Either you choose God and his road map for this life or by default you have chosen Satan and his unholy existence.

Being a clean Temple for God puts us at risk for an attack by God's enemies. Because so many of God's people do not read or know God's word for themselves, they are at risk for being destroyed by God's enemies. The book of Ephesians chapter six in the New Testament outlines the weapons of warfare that Christians must use in order to stand against those who are rebelling against God and his kingdom.

There should be no mystery about our relationship with God. Although there are many things that are beyond our understanding, he has given us a guide in his written word to know him and his Will for our lives. Because God is creativity in its purest form, the manner in which we are related to him could only be materialized by his greatness. He created us in his image. Next he prepared our bodies to become Temples and then deposited a part of his DNA in all who would believe and follow his son Jesus. The DNA that I am referring to is his Holy Spirit. When God looks down from Heaven, He can clearly see those who belong to him and those who do not.

This brings up an important and well debated point of Christian doctrine. It is the question of eternal security. If all Christians have the Holy Spirit dwelling inside of them then they have DNA from the living God. Once you have the DNA of your parent (God in this instance), then it is impossible to stop being a child of his. As with any parent, God has certain expectations for his children. Jesus Christ was sent to be our example on how we are to live and relate to God the Father. Some of these expectations include praying, repenting from sins, baptism, properly administering the sacraments and keeping our Temples (Bodies) clean. The hard part for many Christians is the commitment to keep their Temples clean by maintaining God's standards.

Our relationship to God is a parent/child relationship. Because he loves us, when we sin and defile our Temples, he chastises us. This is what a parent does to bring correction to a child that they love and care about. Because God is a pure and clean spirit, we must come to him as clean as possible. Integrating and trying to be at peace with the world system causes many Christians to be unclean before God. When we do sin and cause our Temples to be unclean, there is a process for us to restore our relationship with God. It is called repentance. If we continue to commit the same sins over and over again, then we cannot really say that we are sorry for our actions and our hearts are not right. Since God is always dealing with our hearts, this is where we get into trouble. Hebrews 6:4-6 describes what happens when we continue to sin after knowing what God expects of us. The Bible declares, "It is impossible for those who have once been enlightened, who have tasted the heavenly gift, who have shared in the Holy Spirit, who have tasted the goodness of the word of God and the powers of the coming age, if they fall away, to be brought back to repentance, because to their loss they are crucifying the Son of God all over again and subjecting him to public disgrace".

How does all of this relate to the subject of eternal security? The doctrine of once saved, always saved, is what most Christian dominations believe. Salvation is every Christian's hope and desire. It is necessary to point out again that Christians have God's DNA (The Holy Spirit) dwelling in them. This is the guarantee of salvation until the day of redemption when God will judge the living and the dead on judgment day. The once saved always saved doctrine comes with expectations. It states, "No matter what you do in this life, you will still go to Heaven". This is the controversial part of the once saved, always saved, doctrine. Some very well educated theologians say that if someone loses their salvation, then they were never really saved. The Bible supports this point of view in the book of Hebrews chapter 6.

Now that we have established that we are children of the living God by DNA, how can it be that some people can lose their salvation? Let us see what the scriptures reveal. There are numerous places in scripture that point out sinful activities that Christians engage in just as those who are not saved. (1 Corinthians 6:9, Galatians 5:19-21,

Hebrews 6:4-6) The Apostle Paul warns of the consequences of continuing in sin after receiving Jesus Christ as your savior. And finally in Matthew 7:21-23 the Lord says, "Not everyone who says to me, 'Lord, Lord,' will enter the kingdom of heaven, but only he who does the will of my Father who is in heaven. Many will say to me on that day, 'Lord, Lord, did we not prophesy in your name and in your name drive out demons and perform many miracles?' Then I will tell them plainly, 'I never knew you. Away from me, you evildoers!'"

In my ministry I often speak to young people who have been brought up with Christian values. When we begin to discuss God and his expectations of his children, many of them do not understand God and his commandments. Modern society teaches a very liberal mindset that allows peaceful co-existence with activities that defile and makes our Temples unclean before God. Many young people are in a rush to have their first sexual experience. They do not have a clue that uniting sexually with someone binds them as one flesh. Rushing into a sexual relationship demonstrates that they do not understand the consequences for breaking God's commandments. They Bible clearly states that they cannot engage in sex until they are married. Modern society has downgraded the importance of the physical and spiritual unity that should only occur in a marriage. When we are discussing Christian values, this is one of the most serious offenses that we can make against God. When we engage in unholy sex, we are defiling not just one Temple but two Temples if we belong to Christ. We must turn to the Lord, repent and ask him to cleanse us of our sins and do not return to them. There is only one circumstance when two people can have sex and be clean before God. It is called marriage.

The Bible has an answer and a solution for most situations that we can get involved in. It has a built in road map that allows us to avoid many of the traps that bring destruction and despair to our lives. As children of the living God, it is our responsibility to follow the road map that God has given to us. Using the Bible in combination with a relationship with the Holy Spirit brings the fruit of the spirit to our lives. The fruit of the Spirit is love, joy, peace, patience, kindness, goodness, faithfulness, gentleness and self-control. Against such things there is no law. Those who belong to Christ Jesus have crucified the sinful nature with its passions and desires. Since we live by the Spirit, let us keep in step with the Spirit. (Galatians 5:22-25) Keeping our Temples clean from the corruption of this world is a top priority. When it comes to keeping our Temples clean, it is our responsibility and a commandment from the Lord.

LOVE AND LIGHT: A CHRISTIAN'S JOURNEY

It is love and being loved that is the highest level of our existence. The Christian adventure and experience in this life is all about sharing the love and light of God. The majority of Christians struggle daily with understanding and demonstrating the love of Christ. For many of us, this is a difficult task. Interacting with the world causes our flesh to react in a way that is not in line with the values that God has commanded us to live by. We understand it intellectually but many of us are powerless to live a life that is pleasing to God. The daily battle of our flesh against our spirit cannot be won by intellect or carnal worldly methods. There are many people who feel unloved in this world. They search for it and never find it. Could it be that they do not know what real love is and are searching for something that is not really love?

Christianity more than any other belief system, has a guide that provides answers and solutions for most situations. Why do we fail so often when it comes to demonstrating the love and light that comes from God? The answer is the flesh. The flesh naturally fights the spirit for control of every situation. A mature Christian realizes when he is operating in the spirit or when he is operating in the flesh. Once a person's actual state (in the flesh or in the spirit) is identified, it is easier to see how they may handle a situation. Let me qualify what I am stating. There are non-Christians who behave in a more spiritual manner than some Christians. The have a belief system that allows them to control their flesh without the spirit of Christ living in them. This is a phenomenon that many atheists use to claim that man can be a moral authority. History has proven over time that this is not true. In every generation there has been a lapse of morality that has destroyed almost every civilization that has ever existed. Man cannot be the ultimate moral authority. His flesh is too susceptible to sin and corruption. Only the spirit of God can truly demonstrate love and light. God uses Christians to project his love and light to the rest of the world. Christians can project love and light because God's spirit lives inside us. Without him, it becomes a form of self – righteousness that does not please him.

When we compare love as it is defined in the Bible, our flesh naturally fights against it. Most humans experience a love that is conditional. This is not the love that emanates from the heart of God. God is eternal and so his love is eternal. It is bigger and more consuming than the love that we understand. Love is clearly defined in the New Testament of the Bible. What some people are searching for to fulfill their lives has nothing to do with the love that is described in the Bible. How can we as Christians explain to people who live in darkness the wonders of God's love? We must be prepared to shine the light from our hearts that is produced by having a loving relationship with God.

In order to experience the love that emanates from the heart of God, people living in the darkness must be brought into the light of Christ. We are the vessels that God uses to accomplish this. 1 Peter 2:9 states, "But ye are a chosen generation, a royal priesthood, a holy nation, a peculiar people; that ye should show forth the praises of him who hath called you out of darkness into his marvelous light". Jesus declared in Matthew 5:14-16, "You are the light of the world. A city on a hill cannot be hidden. Neither do people light a lamp and put it under a bowl. Instead they put it on its stand, and it gives light to everyone in the house. In the same way, let your light shine before men, that they may see your good deeds and praise your Father in heaven".

Without God, we cannot fully understand love. Once we come into his light we can see the enormous gift of love that he has given to us. The power of love is hidden in the cross and blood of Christ. This is God's perfect eternal sacrifice that brings salvation to those who believe in Jesus. Our flesh naturally works against the things of God and love is no exception. There are many passages in the Bible that talk about our lack of love for others and God. In the book of 1 John 4:20-21 the Bible declares, "If anyone says, "I love God," yet hates his brother, he is a liar. For anyone who does not love his brother, whom he has seen, cannot love God, whom he has not seen. And he has given us this command: Whoever loves God must also love his brother". This passage of scripture puts a lot of people on notice. We are all brothers and sisters if we are in Christ. There is no room for racism, bigotry, segregation or anything else that elevates us over one another. We are all to have a servant's heart as our Lord Jesus has shown and taught us.

1 John 4:20-21 is an indictment on the Christian church of today. There is so much division, strife and lack of fellowship among Christians and Christian churches. No wonder many people have doubts about being a part of the Christian experience. The problem again is the flesh that fights against the love that God has commanded that we have for one another. By definition real love cannot change unless sin is involved. Remember, God is love. Whoever does not love, does not know God, because God is love. (1John 4:8)

Let us look at what the Bible has to say about love. "Love is patient, love is kind. It does not envy, it does not boast, it is not proud. It is not rude, it is not self-seeking, is not easily angered. It keeps no record of wrongs. Love does not delight in evil but rejoices with the truth. It always protects, always trusts, always hopes, and always perseveres. Love never fails". (1Corinthians 13:4-8) When we look at the world around us, we see a lot of failures when it comes to love. Why? It is because of our flesh that we fail. Very few people in this world know what love really is. Jesus demonstrated what it is to love. He now expects us to show others what it is to love.

It is very important for us to have a reference to understand love. It is God who created us and designed us with the capacity to love. When we reject him, we also reject the knowledge of how to love.

Not to over simplify but, love is not always easy. Love sometimes hurts. And sometimes love must be tough. Love has parameters. The problems begin when we use our own parameters for love instead of God's, which are the true parameters of love. Let us not get away from the fact that it is God who sets the standards for love and not us.

Because God is light and there is no darkness in him (1 John 1:5), only he can show us the light. Our natural state is to be in the darkness of this world. In fact our daily lives are filled with activities that will try to draw us into darkness. We must continue to walk towards God's light and not be overtaken by the darkness of this world.

This life is filled with choices. God will allow us to choose darkness if we so desire. This is not his Will. In 2 Peter 3:9-14 the Bible states, "The Lord is not slow in keeping his promise, as some understand slowness. He is patient with you, not wanting anyone to perish, but everyone to come to repentance. But the day of the Lord will come like a thief. The heavens will disappear with a roar; the elements will be destroyed by fire, and the earth and everything in it will be laid bare. Since everything will be destroyed in this way, what kind of people ought you to be? You ought to live holy and godly lives as you look forward to the day of God and speed its coming. That day will bring about the destruction of the heavens by fire, and the elements will melt in the heat. But in keeping with his promise we are looking forward to a new heaven and a new earth, the home of righteousness. So then, dear friends, since you are looking forward to this, make every effort to be found spotless, blameless and at peace with him".

A Christian's journey is all about sharing love and walking in God's light. If this is something that does not interest you then Heaven will not be the place for you. Heaven will be a place of love, worship, praise, thanksgiving and peace. It will be nothing like our present existence in this world of darkness. It is God's greatest desire that we all walk toward his light in love and forsake this world of darkness. The life that we live in this world is a wonderful soul-making experience. Our souls will either be conditioned to exist in an environment of love and light or be conditioned to exist in an environment of darkness.

Someone who is selfish, greedy, and full of hatred is not ready for Heaven. If showing and sharing love to others is not a part of someone's earthly life, they will not be conditioned to exist in an environment of love, peace, praise and thanksgiving that will be in Heaven. God will not drag anyone kicking and screaming to Heaven if they do not want to go or are not prepared to go. Fellow Christians, let our love and light shine for the world to see. It is only through this demonstration of obedience to God that the world knows that we belong to him.

THE JOY OF BEING A CHRISTIAN

Christians possess a joy that cannot be surpassed. The knowledge that whatever we have done in this life is forgiven is truly astounding. This is because we put our faith and confidence in Jesus Christ. Don't get me wrong. Some people have done some very horrible things in their lives and looking at it in the natural, there is no way for them to be forgiven. Thanks to our Lord and Savior Jesus who gave his life to pay for ALL sin. It is the guilt of our sin that steals our joy. There are many people in the world who are not happy. They have all the material wealth and even good physical health yet they are still unhappy. There is something missing in their lives. It is the guilt of their sin that they must deal with. There is only one way to effectively deal with this and that is to turn their lives over to Jesus as their Lord and Savior. Once this is done, the guilt of their sin is lifted and forgiven.

Unfortunately for some of us the reality of the forgiveness of sin is not enough to experience the joy, peace and happiness that come with a relationship with the Lord. The acceptance of Jesus as Lord and Savior is not complete. Although some of us are saved and going to Heaven, the guilt of our sins remain in our emotions. This is an area of relationship with God and the church that needs to be improved. This is why it is so important to not forsake the assembling of the saints on a regular basis. When we are in fellowship with other believers, we can teach the difference between our guilt before God and the guilt of our conscious. Once God justifies us, we are forgiven. It is then that the sanctification process can begin to heal our conscious.

With this forgiveness comes an important understanding. Once we confess our sin to God, forgiveness is granted and God allows joy and peace to enter our life. The consequences for sin however must still be accounted for. Let us take murder for example. If someone commits a murder, they can be granted forgiveness in God's system of justice. This person still has an opportunity to confess and repent of their sin. There are earthly consequences that may still apply. The obvious consequence is going to jail or even the death penalty. In either event the person does not lose his place in eternity with God.

This is the eternal security that Christianity offers that no other belief system can. Knowing that this life is temporary and then we must enter eternity scares many people. An important benefit of being a Christian is that a road map for this life and the life to come is provided in the Holy Bible.

Many people take issue with this doctrine. How can someone like Adolf Hitler be forgiven for all the lives that he took and destroyed? According to God's system of justice, it is still possible for someone like Hitler to be saved. As we read the account of what happened to him, it is very unlikely that he confessed his sins and repented to God. Without a confession of sin and a truly repentant heart, there is no forgiveness of sin in God's system of justice. This is an area of Christian doctrine that many people fail to understand. There are many people professing to be Christians. What they do not realize is that it is their hearts and actions that will be judged and not their speech. We see it on a daily basis that people say one thing but in their hearts and actions do the opposite. The truth of the matter is, they are fooling themselves. This kind of lifestyle will certainly lead to eternal separation from God. This falls under the sin of being a hypocrite.

Looking at the world today and seeing its rush to destroy itself is an indication of a lack of relationship with God. Taking, believing and understanding God's written word provides a road map to peace and a joy in our lives. God's word contains strict boundaries to live by. It demonstrates how to live with peace and joy in your life even when things are bad. It is the constant renewing of our minds with the word of God that enables us to stand in times of trouble. The Bible is clear about the trials that we all must face. It is how we respond to these trials that brings glory or shame to our relationship with God. Too many times we are tested to see if we will stand and hold our values but fail. Failing is not a bad thing unless we do not learn from it. Failure by the world's standards is so different when compared to God's standards. When we fail God, he is there to restore us and teach us important eternal truths that will be with us forever. Failure in the world system is usually accompanied by shame, ruin and ridicule. For the most part, there is no system of forgiveness and restoration back to your previous status in the world. You are marked negatively for life.

Let us take a look at a common example. Someone is convicted of stealing and sentenced to prison for a number of years. They served their time, learned from their mistake and have truly reformed. Once they are released from prison after paying their debt to society, society does not restore them back to a position of trust. Instead they are marked for life and in most cases will never have another opportunity to have any substantial position in society. They are stuck in a cycle that will eventually lead them back into the prison system. Because they are marked for life and cannot hold a position that society trusts and admires, they will normally turn back to crime as a way of life. In general, the world system is unforgiving. Of course there are exceptions.

As Christians we are constantly challenged to abandon our values and make peace with the world and its values. This is where the battle lines are drawn in the spiritual war. Anytime that Christians acquiesce and violate God's commandments to have peace with the world, we are putting our trust and faith in something else. This is often referred to as idolatry. This has been happening since the beginning of time. Christians are constantly being drawn into idolatry. They put their trust and faith in other things rather than God. As stated earlier, there are consequences for sin.

Let us take a closer look at the consequences of sin that produces a guilty heart and mind. Having guilt as a part of our lives by definition, robs us of our peace of mind. A guilty mind can never experience the joy that God designed to be a part of our being. It is this guilt that separates us from God. Thank God for his son Jesus that is able to restore our relationship with him. He is the key to joy and peace in our lives. The ability to confess and repent of our sin is a wonderful part of being a Christian. All sins are covered by the blood of Christ. Liars, Cheaters, Thieves and even Murderers can have joy and peace restored in their lives through a relationship with Christ. There are too many instances of violations of God's laws to mention. Isn't it wonderful to know that God's system of justice can handle any and all of them? In the end there will be an accounting for the deeds done while in the body. (2 Corinthians 5:10) Even the most devout Christian will have to give an account of his life. God's system of justice will deal with what is in our hearts. Our hearts will be the witness to show God what kind of relationship that we have with him. It will tell our deepest secrets. It will also tell us of the joy and peace that we have in him or the lack of it.

The knowledge of keeping our Temples clean is an important part of the peace and joy that God provides us. Our bodies which are the Temples of the living God must be kept clean for him to dwell in. Can you imagine inviting our natural parents to stay with us and our homes are unclean? This is what many of us do. We must take the importance of keeping our bodies clean seriously. Do you want to be ashamed of how you are living and then invite God to be there with you? This is another part of sin that brings guilt. We stop honoring God by keeping our bodies (Temples) unclean. In the spirit war we are constantly under attack to steal our joy and peace. Knowing this we must put on the full armor of God and be ready to engage our enemies at all times. Not being holy (clean by God's standards) puts us at a disadvantage when trying to fight in the spirit war.

The spirit war is all about the world and its destiny trying to include us with them. The world is gambling on the belief that there is no God, no judgment and no hell. They want us to also gamble with our souls. Christian amnesia is a Christian's worse enemy. We forget who we are, where we come from and where we are supposed to be going. The world and its allure keep many of us in bondage. The bondage of sin creates the guilt that keeps us separated from the peace and joy of a relationship with God.

As God reveals more and more of the mystery of creation and our relationship with him, we can have confidence in the peace and joy for all those who put their faith in his son Jesus Christ. The joy of a heart that is not filled with guilt is one of the most important promises of God. The perfect peace that can only come from a relationship with him is revealed in the Gospel of Jesus Christ.

Joy and peace in this life can only come from God. He designed us and made us to be incomplete without a relationship with him.

Trying to achieve peace and joy in our lives without God will always fail. This life was never designed for us to be separated from him. As we see our society and the world turning away from God, the more we see less and less of his joy and peace.

A NOTE FROM THE AUTHOR

The Christian experience is made more difficult because of certain traditions and doctrines of some churches. The vast number of denominations within Christianity speaks directly to this problem. The process of finding a church that is Christ centered rather than man centered is becoming more and more difficult. The phrase "Church Hopping" comes to mind. There are Christians that visit a number of churches within their own denomination and some outside of their denomination trying to find a place to fit in. The reason why people engage in church hopping varies. One reason that people engage in trying different churches is that there is something missing or not quite right in the churches that they attend. Some people church hop because of the music, pageantry, traditions or teaching that makes them feel good. Other people leave a good biblical, Christ-centered church because the church dared to discipline them or someone in their family. Church leaders experience a tendency towards church hopping when counseling people against living together outside of marriage or counseling couples contemplating divorce. People will go to the church down the street where the pastor will give them his blessing for sinful lifestyles (Not God's blessing of course). It is a case of selective Christianity where people try to find which church will allow them to remain in their sins. People get angry, offended (emotionally, not biblically) when the church teaches unpopular things. Some people choose churches because of their location, time of service, stained glass windows, personality or oratorical skills of the pastor, friendships and family relationships. Sadly the search for sound Christian doctrine is overlooked. Because many Christians are not being properly educated, they find themselves constantly searching for the perfect church.

As Christians, we all must find a church where we fit in. This is especially true for new converts. In my years in ministry I have found that this process could take some time. Watching and observing the social structure of a church will provide insight over time about the spiritual condition of that church. A relationship with a church can be similar to a relationship with a person. With some people that you meet, it seems as though you have known them all your life and it feels good to be around them. With others, you know instantly that you will not be close. It is the same when choosing a church.

When it comes to choosing a church, our relationship with the Lord plays a very important part. Some Christians claim that it is God himself that directs them to be involved with a particular church. I believe that this is true. What I also believe is that God may direct someone to a particular church to learn some spiritual truth or lesson. In other words, the experience of being directed to a particular church may not be for us to stay there long. It may just mean that God has something there for our spiritual growth and development. Many church leaders are controlling and want members to be obedient to every tradition of the church, even if the church is not Christ centered. In some instances, it may seem to be a negative experience. In the end we find that the Lord allowed us to experience this to grow us spiritually.

An important experience that sometimes occurs while searching for a church is that you infuse it with a spirit of revival. Many churches arrive at a place of complacency and dullness. They do the same things over and over and lose the spirit of excitement for the things of God. As a newcomer to a church in this condition, you may be able to breathe some fresh air into it. This reminds me of the argument on term limits. The church is supposed to be a living growing organism that develops future leaders. In some cases when the same people are in charge for too long, the church loses its edge and direction. In today's changing world we need to train future leaders to maintain kingdom principles and not get caught up in the entertainment, money and acceptance of sinful lifestyles of some of its members. Because of the lure of money and power, some churches have become desensitized to sin. They are willing to accept members who openly live sinful lifestyles and have no intention of changing. This is where an outsider can be a great benefit to that church. If the church leadership is open to correction, then a visit from someone searching for a good Christian home could start a revival in that congregation.

As we mature in our relationship with the Lord, it becomes more and more obvious when church leaders are following traditions that are not Christ centered. It is then necessary to find a way to reveal this to church leadership without causing harm to your relationship with that church. If church leadership is not receptive, then a choice must be made to either stay and accept false traditions and doctrine or leave that particular church. When this happens often over a short period of time, this can be referred to as "Church Hopping".

The more mature you are in your faith, the more prone you may be to Church Hopping until you find the right church. Church leaders frown upon this but Christ-centered church leaders want you serving God somewhere even if it is not with their church. As a child of the living God, one should not feel bad because there is no feeling of joy and peace in a particular church. Continue to seek God's guidance until he puts you in the church that you belong. Visiting and looking at different churches is another part of your spiritual growth and development. Do not settle until God introduces you to your church family.

Attending a good New testament Church is extremely important for the nourishment of a Christian's Temple (Body) Now that we have the knowledge that our bodies are Temples of the living God, we must continually provide the proper nourishment for it in addition to keeping it clean. This includes the normal food products that we need in vitamins and minerals but also spiritual food. Jesus set the standard for all who will follow him. When Jesus was being tempted by Satan in the desert after fasting for forty days and forty nights, he was hungry. Satan tempted him by saying, "If you are the son of God, tell these stones to become bread". Jesus replied to him, "It is written that man does not live on bread alone but on every word that comes from the mouth of God". (Matthew 4:4) This is the first reference that the word of God is the spiritual food that all Christians need to nourish their bodies.

Understanding that spiritual nourishment is essential for growth and development, what we eat becomes critical. Because there are so many denominations within Christianity, there are many different menus that people are eating from. Many of these menus do not include the word of God as Jesus described in Matthew 4:4. There are church leaders that are feeding their followers the wrong food. This is apparent in that there are so many different doctrines, traditions and rituals within Christianity. All of them cannot be right so therefore some must be wrong. This raises the question of who is right and who is wrong? Now it becomes the responsibility of each believer to know the word of God independently on their own.

For centuries the word of God was hidden from the general public. Whatever church leaders disseminated to the people was thought to be from God. Over the centuries it has been revealed that some of these church leaders were changing and using the word of God to control, coerce and instill fear into people. By doing this they were able to get people to do the things that they wanted. In some instances these church leaders actually used fear and guilt to enslave the minds of people. The practice of controlling people by using what appears to be the word of God is a common practice that continues today. There are basic principles that can never change. Principles such as being a humble servant, caring for the poor, avoiding sexual perversions, holiness, forgiveness etc. can never change.

Proper food that leads to a closer relationship with God is often not on many church menus. Instead what we find are menus that bring you closer to a relationship with a church and its leaders, not God. Some church leaders make it seem as though you must go through them in order to have a relationship with God. Jesus tells us plainly that no one comes to the Father except through him. (John 14:6) Finding a church that is serving a proper diet for Christians is becoming difficult. The world in its present condition makes it almost impossible for Christians to live on a healthy diet of God's word.

As a born again Christian, we have one life. It is not segmented into different behaviors because the world requires this of us. Our primary focus is to serve and glorify God. Submitting to worldly authority now requires a thorough knowledge of the word of God in order not to lose our Christian identity. The Apostle Paul warned us in 2 Timothy 4:12-15 that we will be persecuted for practicing our faith. Paul states, "In fact, everyone who wants to live a Godly life in Christ Jesus will be persecuted, while evil men and imposters will go from bad to worse, deceiving and being deceived. But as for you, continue in what you have learned and become convinced of, because you know those from whom you learned it, and how from infancy you have known the Holy Scriptures which are able to make you wise for salvation through faith in Christ Jesus".

When we depart from nourishing our bodies with the word of God both individually and corporately, we start feeding on what the world system gives us. We become sick and anemic lacking spiritual discernment and power. This is the fate of the world that denies Christ.

Made in the USA
Columbia, SC
29 November 2024